IT'S ALL IN YOUR HEAD

A Guide to Understanding Your Brain and Boosting Your Brain Power

BY SUSAN L. BARRETT

Edited by Pamela Espeland
Illustrations by Jackie Urbanovic

free spirit
PUBLiSHiNG®

Works
for kids®

D0092484

Library of Congress Cataloging-in-Publication Data

Barrett, Susan L. (Susan Laura), 1957–
　　It's all in your head : a guide to understanding your brain and boosting your brain power / by Susan L. Barrett ; edited by Pamela Espeland ; illustrations by Jackie Urbanovic. — Rev. ed.
　　　　p.　cm.
　　Includes bibliographical references and index.
　　Summary: Discusses the physiology and evolution of the brain, definitions and measuring of intelligence, problem solving, and other related topics. Also includes suggestions for further reading and activities for stimulating creative thinking and other intellectual abilities.
　　ISBN 0-915793-45-8
　　1. Brain—Juvenile literature.　2. Cognition—Juvenile literature. 3. Memory—Juvenile literature. [1. Brain　2. Intellect.] I. Espeland, Pamela, 1951–　　. II. Urbanovic, Jackie, Ill.　III. Title.
QP376.B36　　1992
153—dc20
　　　　　　　　　　　　　　　　　　　　　　　　　　92-18090
　　　　　　　　　　　　　　　　　　　　　　　　　　　　CIP
　　　　　　　　　　　　　　　　　　　　　　　　　　　　AC

Definitions of *brain* and *mind* on page 5 reprinted by permission. From the Merriam-Webster Dictionary 1974 by Merriam-Webster Inc., publisher of the Merriam-Webster® Dictionaries.

Excerpt from "The Early Mental Traits of Three Hundred Geniuses" on page 30 by Catherine Morris Cox, in *Genetic Studies of Genius*, Volume II, edited by Lewis M. Terman (Stanford, CA: Stanford University Press, 1926). Reprinted by permission of the publisher.

Cover and text design by MacLean & Tuminelly

20　19　18　17　16　15　14　13　12　11
Printed in the United States of America

Free Spirit Publishing Inc.
217 Fifth Avenue North, Suite 200
Minneapolis, MN 55401-1299
(612) 338-2068
help4kids@freespirit.com
www.freespirit.com

For my family, Scott, Casey, Kyle, and Connor

As we travel through the journey of life,
may we continue to discover the joy of learning together.

CONTENTS

> "The Brain—is wider than the Sky—
> For—put them side by side—
> The one the other will contain
> with ease—and You—beside."
>
> Emily Dickinson, American poet

INTRODUCTION

Your brain has been custom-made for you. It's an original. One of a kind. And it came fully equipped with everything you'll ever need (and then some!).

But one thing it *didn't* come with is an instruction manual. So it's up to you to figure out how to use your brain, how to make the most of it, and how to get it to do what you want it to do.

Does that sound like a tall order? It is! Especially since your brain has unlimited potential. What that means is...there's no end to what you and your brain can do.

This book is for kids like you who are interested in exploring the possibilities—and capabilities—of their brains. Maybe you've already noticed that there are lots of books and magazine articles about the scientific features of the brain. The fact is, you could spend eight hours a day for the rest of your life reading about the brain, and you still wouldn't get to everything written about *one single year's* worth of research and findings.

So it's no surprise that this book won't tell you everything about the brain. No book could ever do that. But it *will* tell you some things you want to know.

How do we know what *you* want to know? Because we interviewed more than 450 kids ages 8-16 from all over the United States. What we learned was that most kids were interested in investigating the mysteries of the mind—the "unknowns." Here are some of the questions they wanted answers to:

- ✆ Why do we dream, and what happens when we dream?

- ✆ What does the brain do when we are asleep?

- ✆ Can eating certain foods make me smarter?

- ✆ What is déjà vu all about?

- ✆ Is it true that people have a sixth sense?

- ✆ Why does my brain sometimes play tricks on me?

- ✆ Is it possible to increase or extend the powers of the mind?

- What is intuition, and how can we use it?
- Can a computer ever work as well as the brain?
- Can the mind go beyond the senses—and beyond time and space?

One way to approach these topics is by first examining some of the facts about the brain—the "knowns." Here are more questions kids thought were worth exploring:

- Why are some people more intelligent than others?
- What is an I.Q. test, and what does it test?
- How did the brain evolve?
- What goes on inside the brain?
- How do we learn and remember things?
- What are the differences between the right brain and the left brain?
- What is creativity, and where does it come from?
- Is it possible to become *more* intelligent and/or *more* creative?
- How many ways can people be intelligent?
- How does the brain store our memories?
- Where does intelligence come from, our genes or our environment?
- What can I do to take care of my brain?

Have *you* ever wondered about these questions? If so, you've come to the right place. Maybe you've wondered about other questions. Maybe someday you'll write your own book about the brain.

The only limitations on your brain are the ones *you* put on it. Your brain may only be a thousand cubic centimeters in volume—about the size of a grapefruit—but it packs a LOT of power! We hope that you'll use this power to discover *your* true talents and abilities. You may even find some you didn't know you had.

THE BRAIN HAS MORE ANSWERS
THAN YOU HAVE QUESTIONS.

**"Do what you can with what you have
where you are."**

Theodore Roosevelt, twenty-sixth President of the
United States, author of 17 books, big-game hunter, and
the person the Teddy Bear was named after

Brain vs. Mind

In this book, we talk about both the "brain" and the "mind." They're not necessarily the same, although the two terms are often used interchangeably. If you want to get picky, here are the definitions:

▶ The *brain* is "the part of the vertebrate nervous system that is the organ of thought and nervous coordination, is made up of nerve cells and their fibers, and is enclosed in the skull."

In other words, it's that lump of stuff inside your head that thinks and coordinates all of your bodily functions. It's a *thing* that can be weighed and measured and looked at and studied.

▶ The *mind* is "the part of an individual that feels, perceives, thinks, wills, and especially reasons."

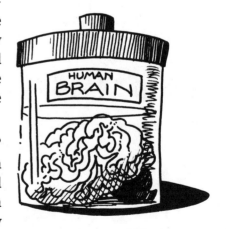

If that sounds a bit looser than the definition of the brain, it is. It's generally believed that the mind resides in the brain. But the brain isn't the same as the mind—not exactly.

What's the difference? Well, the brain is an organ, a part of the body; the mind isn't. A scientist can put a brain in a jar, but nobody can put a *mind* in a jar.

Recently, some scientists have been working on creating a new model of the mind which connects brain and mind research. Scientists who study the biology of the brain are becoming more interested in studying the mind. And psychologists who study the mind are now exploring the biology of the brain. So far, they think that the mind is not one large neural network, but a collection of small units that work together. They hope to invent a "thinking machine" that mimics the human brain.

These daring scientists (known as *connectionists*) are creating startling new theories of how the mind works. Perhaps their findings will change the way we think about ourselves and the world. What do *you* think about this new science?

"If my heart could do my thinking, would my brain begin to feel?"

Van Morrison, singer, songwriter, and musician

Brain Stats

- Each and every second of your life, several billion bits of information pass through your brain.
- Messages within your brain travel through trillions of neural connections at speeds up to 250 miles per hour.
- Your brain generates 25 watts of power while you're awake—enough to illuminate a light bulb.
- Your brain uses 20% of your body's energy, but it makes up only 2% of your body's weight.
- You use only 1%, 2%, 5%, 10%, or 20% of your brain's capacity (depending on which scientist you talk to!).
- The brain has about 100 billion neurons.

"The total number of connections within the vast network of the brain's neuronal system is truly astronomical—greater than the number of particles in the known universe."

Richard Restak, M.D., author of *The Brain*

Brain Facts

- The brain of a 6-month-old child is already 1/2 its adult weight.

- The brain of a 2 1/2-year-old child is already 3/4 its adult weight.

- The brain of a 5-year-old child is already 9/10 its adult weight.

- Human brains are getting bigger. Your brain weighs about half a pound more than your great-grandparent's brain did when he or she was your age.

The heaviest known normal brain weighed 4.43 pounds. It belonged to Ivan Turgenev, a Russian writer who died in 1883. His brain was more than a pound heavier than the average male brain of his time.

So far, no one has come up with a robot or a computer that has a brain as good as ours.

HOW THE BRAIN EVOLVED AND WHAT THE DIFFERENT PARTS DO

Millions of years ago, the brain was just a clump of cells called *ganglia*. It was barely a brain at all, and it wasn't very sophisticated. The problem was, it had to get more sophisticated if the life forms that existed back then were going to survive, evolve, and adapt to their changing environment.

Lucky for us, it did. As various life forms moved from water-breathers to air-breathers, from swimmers to crawlers (and some to flyers), their brains grew better and better.

Today we actually have three brains in one. Each is a sort of "control center," with its own jobs to do. Let's explore these control centers and find out why they're so important.

The Brain Stem

The brain stem is the oldest and most primitive part of the brain. It evolved more than 500 million years ago—before mammals. It's sometimes called by other names: the "reptilian brain," the "R complex," the "lower brain," or the "hind brain."

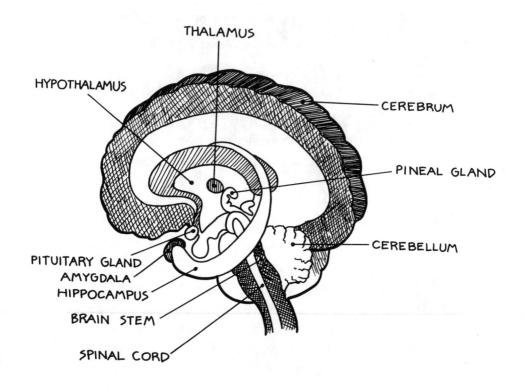

THALAMUS

HYPOTHALAMUS

CEREBRUM

PINEAL GLAND

CEREBELLUM

PITUITARY GLAND
AMYGDALA
HIPPOCAMPUS

BRAIN STEM

SPINAL CORD

The brain stem is really an extension of the spinal cord. The swelling on it is called the *medulla oblongata*. The medulla oblongata regulates your life-support systems—things your body does without thinking. Your heart is beating, you're breathing, your blood is circulating, and your stomach is digesting the last meal you ate because your medulla oblongata is at work.

The *limbic system* evolved around 250 million years ago. It surrounds the brain stem like a donut. It used to be called the "smell brain" because of its direct connections to smell and taste receptors. Now we know that it also performs many other functions, including memory storage. The so-called "mood-altering" drugs affect the limbic system, which is why the not-too-smart people who take them feel emotionally high or low.

The limbic system is made up of the *thalamus*, the *hypothalamus*, the *pituitary gland*, the *pineal gland*, the *amygdala*, and the *hippocampus*.

- **Your thalamus** monitors and sorts out messages from your senses so you don't get confused.

- **Your hypothalamus** houses your emotions and regulates your body temperature. (Without it, we'd be cold-blooded, like the reptiles.) It lets you know when you're hungry or thirsty, controls your blood pressure, and is the source of your sexual feelings.

- **Your pituitary gland** controls the release of hormones which enable your body to produce energy out of the food you eat.

- **Your pineal gland** is responsible for the rate at which your body grows and matures. It's like a biological clock that's activated by light.

- **Your amygdala** can trigger either angry aggression or docility, depending on the situation you're in and which part is affected.

- **Your hippocampus** forms and stores new memories. (Scientists think it may even have more responsibilities that are still undiscovered.)

Another system is located at the upper part of the brain stem. Called the RAS, for **R**eticular **A**ctivating **S**ystem, it acts like a master switch or alarm bell, alerting your brain to information coming in from the senses. Without it, you'd be in a coma.

The RAS, which is about the size of your little finger, also acts like a sieve, allowing certain messages to pass through to the thinking part of your brain faster than others. For example, if you were in a house that caught fire, your RAS would react to that information more quickly than to the sound of your neighbor's lawn mower starting up. Somehow it knows the difference between what's important and what's trivial.

Your RAS is useful in still another way: It helps to filter out sensory stimuli so you can concentrate. Imagine that you're trying to read a book in a busy shopping mall. Your RAS will filter out the crowd noises—but if someone calls your name, you'll hear it.

Tennis pros like Martina Navratilova and John McEnroe develop control over their RAS. When they're standing on the court at Wimbledon, focusing on the serve that's coming at them like lightning, they must be able to shut out everything else around them. The RAS comes to the rescue!

The Cerebellum

The two-layered bulge which sticks out of the brain stem is called the *cerebellum*, or "mini-brain." The cerebellum coordinates your muscles so you aren't a total klutz.

Posture, movement, and the sense of balance are all housed in the cerebellum. We can thank it for making it possible for us to bounce, throw, and catch balls. It helps us make accurate and delicate movements, such as picking up a glass of juice without spilling it. Plus some researchers think that the cerebellum may have something to do with emotional development.

When you run a race or practice the piano, it's your cerebellum that shifts your muscles into automatic pilot. The more you practice, the better it gets. Think about how hard the cerebellums of people like Michael Jordan and the Olympic athletes must be working!

The Cerebrum

The cerebrum is the newest and largest of our three brains. It's called the "forebrain," the "upper brain," and (for obvious reasons) the "new brain." The way it evolved is especially interesting. Millions of years ago, this part of the brain was nothing but a sight-and-smell machine that helped animals to locate food and escape from their enemies. In amphibians, it gradually grew a surface layer called the *cortex* (which means "outer rind," like the rind of an orange).

As animals got smarter, the cortex got larger and became the *neocortex* (or "new cortex"). But the skull didn't grow as quickly, so the neocortex had to find a way to fit inside it. It did this by crumpling into wrinkles and folds called *convolutions*.

Your cerebrum is full of convolutions. In fact, if you pulled it out of your head and spread it flat, it would be about as large as the Sunday comics. Your cortex covers your whole cerebrum and is about as thick as a tongue depressor.

What does your cerebrum do? Plenty. You could call it your "thinking cap." Because of it, you're able to reason and solve problems. It houses your intellect, your memory, your language skills, and your ability to understand symbols (including numbers and the letters of the alphabet). Plus it makes decisions—after first comparing new information it receives with information that's already stored inside your head.

Your cerebrum makes up about 85 percent of your brain's total mass and is divided into two halves, or *hemispheres*. Each hemisphere contains different networks of cells that receive, store, and retrieve information. When people refer to the "left brain" and the "right brain," what they mean is the two hemispheres of the cerebrum.

There's been a lot of talk in recent years about left-brain and right-brain functions. We'll get around to that topic later. (If you can't wait, turn to pages 45–48.)

"We don't know one millionth of one percent about anything."

Thomas Edison, inventor of the electric light bulb and the phonograph, holder of over 1,000 patents—and he attended school for only three months

If you want to know more about the evolution of the brain and its inner workings, read:

* *The Amazing Brain* by Robert Ornstein and Richard F. Thompson (Boston: Houghton-Mifflin Company, 1986).

* *The Brain and Nervous System* by Brian R. Ward (New York: Franklin Watts Company, 1981).

* *The World of the Brain* by Alvin and Virginia B. Silverstein (New York: Morrow Jr. Books, 1986).

** *The Brain* by Richard M. Restak, M.D. (New York: Warner Books, Inc., 1988).

Note: Throughout this book, we'll be referring you to other resources—places to go to find out more. One star (*) means an easy-to-read book. Two stars (**) mean a not-so-easy to read book. Three stars (***) mean a book that's hard to read but worth the effort.

A LOOK INSIDE YOUR BRAIN

On the surface, most human brains look pretty much the same: light-pink-and-grayish-white, wrinkled, and squishy. Brains can vary in size and weight, but the average male brain weighs 49 ounces and the average female brain weighs 44 ounces.

Some people have smaller brains, while others have real whoppers. But *brain weight and size have nothing to do with intelligence.* In fact, "small-brained" people may actually be more intelligent than "big-brained" people. (Einstein's brain wasn't unusually large, although it was different in at least one other way from most people's. More about that later.) In any case, it's what's *inside* the brain that counts.

Imagine what it would be like if you could look inside your own brain...if you could shut your eyes and peer inward with electron-microscope super-vision... closer...closer...closer at the individual brain cells....Here's some of what you'd see.

Neurons, Axons, and Dendrites

You were born with about 100 billion brain cells. People used to think that the more brain cells you had, the smarter you were, but now we know that this isn't true.

About 10-50 billion of these are nerve cells called *neurons*. A neuron is a basic unit of the brain. It's as complex as a small computer. Like a mini-information processing system, it sends and receives thousands of messages in the form of nerve impulses. A single neuron can handle as many as 50,000 messages per minute! Just as no two brains are alike, no two neurons are alike. Each has its own irregular shape, sort of like a tiny octopus with tentacles.

A neuron consists of a cell body (which contains the nucleus), long fibers called *axons*, and short, branching fibers called *dendrites*.

How Does It All Work?

First, the neuron receives a message. Then it processes the message inside the cell body. Then it sends it out to other neurons by way of the axons.

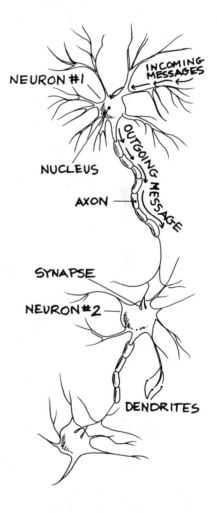

When a message travels along the length of an axon at up to 100 miles per hour, it comes close to "touching" the dendrites of the neighboring neurons. But it never *quite* touches them. Instead, the message is transmitted chemically across an infinitesimally small gap called a *synapse*.

Is a synapse just a hole in your brain? Hardly. Synapses make it possible for neurons to communicate with one another. (Think of a synapse as a bridge.) Scientists believe that synapses somehow "decide" whether or not a message gets transmitted. (Now think of it as a "smart" bridge.) They also believe that synapses are where learning and memory occur. So they're *very* important. (Think of it as the Golden Gate bridge.)

A lot of action takes place whenever a message is transmitted. Each message starts off as an electrical impulse. Then it changes into a chemical signal. Then it changes back into an electrical impulse. All within a split second! Right now, while you're reading this book, up to one million impulses could be flashing through your brain at speeds of up to 250 miles per hour!

The Cosmic Dance

Remember that you only use a portion of your brain's total capacity. What if you could activate the whole thing at once? Dr. Pyotr Anokhin has tried to calculate the number of synaptic connections possible within a normal human brain. He estimates a total of 1 followed by 6,213,710 miles of typewritten zeros—and he thinks this figure might be too low!

Plus: Whenever you learn something new, this creates even more links between your neurons. The number of neurons stay the same, but they have more ways to share messages.

According to Dr. Barbara Clark, author of *Growing Up Gifted*, a stimulating environment can cause changes in the chemical makeup of the neurons. The strength and speed of the activity at the synapses actually increase. It may be that "smart" people are smart simply because they have better synaptic connections between their brain cells.

An environment full of learning opportunities also affects other brain cells called *glial cells*. These cells "glue" your brain together. Unlike neurons, glial cells can split in two and duplicate themselves. When this happens, axons can push through and make connections to other neurons. The richer your environment, the faster your glial cells split.

Remember we promised you more on Einstein's brain? Here it is: Dr. Marian Diamond, a California brain scientist, located Albert Einstein's frozen brain in a box in a freezer in Kansas. She and her associates wanted to know why Einstein was such a mathematical genius. They managed to get pieces of his brain and discovered that the math thinking part of his brain had more glial cells than most people. So Einstein had more synaptic connections.

Electrical impulses! Messages coming and going! Multiplying synapses! Splitting cells! And you thought things were pretty quiet up there! Now imagine that these messages are tiny lights, and that you can see them zipping through your brain. What does it look like?

A million, billion stars doing a brilliant cosmic dance!

Brain Scanners: Peering Through the Skull

CATs, MRIs, PETs, SQUIDs....These may sound like things you'd find at a pet shop. In reality, they are the most powerful new devices we have for seeing the brain at work. Let's take a look at what they can do.

👁 **CAT Scan.** CAT stands for **C**omputer-**A**ssisted **T**omography. This is an older method which produces pictures of the brain's structure, but can't distinguish between a live brain and a dead one.

👁 **MRI**. MRI stands for **M**agnetic **R**esonance **I**maging. This test can snap detailed pictures of the brain, but it can't detect brain functions.

👁 **PET Scan.** PET stands for **P**ositron **E**mission **T**omography. This newer way to explore the brain tracks blood flow, a proxy for brain activity. First, a person is injected with radioactive glucose. The glucose mixes with the blood and goes to the brain. The more active a part of the brain is, the more glucose it uses. PET sensors pinpoint the source of heightened activity and send it through computers to show the neural hot spots.

👁 **SQUID.** SQUID stands for **S**uperconductivity **Q**uantum **I**nterference **D**evice. This technique picks up magnetic fields, a mark of brain activity. (When neurons fire, they create an electrical current. Electrical fields induce magnetic fields, and magnetic changes indicate neural activity.)

Each type of scan has its strengths and weaknesses. More importantly, each helps us to look into the skull and see the brain at work. They can be used to learn about brain organization and make sense of that jungle of neurons in your head.

For example, with SQUID, scientists found that the brain hears loud sounds in a totally different place from quiet sounds. Using a PET scanner, other researchers discovered that people use lots of mental energy when learning something new, but the energy level drops after they have practiced it awhile.

These scans demonstrate that the brain is made up of many "specialists." Different regions process different information. Knowing this can open new windows into the brain. Scientists are busy learning about thoughts and emotions and their importance to intelligence and language. Isn't it exciting to realize that we're entering a new field where scientists will actually be able to "read your mind"?

▲▲▲▲▲▲▲▲▲▲▲▲▲▲▲▲▲▲▲

If you want to know more about how your brain sends and receives messages, read:

*   *The Brain and Nervous System* by Schoolhouse Press, Inc. (Englewood Cliffs, NJ: Silver Burdett, 1987).

*** *Brain, Mind, and Behavior* by Floyd E. Bloom, Arlyne Lazerson, and Laura Hofstadter, 2nd edition (New York: W.H. Freeman and Company, 1988).

▼▼▼▼▼▼▼▼▼▼▼▼▼▼▼▼▼▼▼

DEFINING INTELLIGENCE

You may think you're smart...but you're even smarter than you think. You have the potential for understanding the nature of your own intelligence—and changing it. There's no limit to how much your brain can learn. In fact, the more you know, the more you CAN know!

"You can be smarter tomorrow than you are today. The mind can stretch—it can be strengthened, toned, and conditioned to perform miracles for you. Your mind can carry you into the 21st century even before the second millennium."

Marilyn vos Savant, author and consultant; according to the *Guinness Book of World Records*, she has the highest I.Q. ever recorded: 230!

Does "Smart" Equal "Intelligent"?

For decades, the brain has been called "the organ of intelligence." When you hear someone say, "What a brain!" or "She's brainy!", what they usually mean is that the person is smart.

But is "smartness" the same as "intelligence"? Can we define one by the other? If you're not sure, you're not alone. Scientists are stumped when it comes to deciding on a definition of intelligence—especially human intelligence. (Intelligence is usually much easier to recognize than it is to define.)

Some say it's "the ability to learn and apply what has been learned." But almost every creature on Earth—not just humans—can learn and act on the basis of what it learns. Some say it's "using what has been learned to solve problems." But monkeys can do this, too. Still others say it's "the ability to judge well, comprehend well, and reason well." Now we're getting somewhere! Most experts agree that our ability to think and reason is what sets us apart from the other animals and makes us special.

One of the most recent definitions states that "intelligence is the result of all the functions of the human brain...a combination of physical, emotional, mental, and spiritual energies." That about covers it.

Sternberg's Definition

Robert Sternberg, a leading authority on intelligence, interviewed hundreds of people and asked them what they considered to be the "characteristics of intelligence." He came up with three very general ones:

1. Practical problem-solving ability,

2. Verbal activity (being able to recognize, understand, and reason with words), and

3. Social competence (or "human relations skills"—the ability to communicate with other people).

Sternberg also wrote his own definition of intelligence: "goal-directed, adaptive behavior."

■ ■ ■ ■ ■ ■ ■ ■ ■ ■ ■ ■ ■ ■ ■

HOW KIDS DEFINE INTELLIGENCE

We asked more than 450 kids ages 8–16 to give us their definitions of intelligence. Here's what some of them said:

◆ "I think intelligence is a high level of thinking that all ages can do. Creativity is a BIG part of it." *Megan, 10*

◆ "To me, intelligence means being able to stretch your mind further." *Don, 11*

◆ "Being able to learn things on your own." *Kari, 13*

◆ "Being able to learn, understand and apply a theory or idea." *Steve, 14*

◆ "Being able to understand yourself." *Katie, 10*

◆ "Being creative and a good thinker." *Kelly, 10*

◆ "Does it mean being more logical and highly advanced?" *Brenda, 11*

◆ "To me, intelligence is creativity." *Wendy, 9*

◆ "I think that intelligence is the knowledge someone has. Intelligence can be logical or creative." *Rudy, 11*

◆ "Intelligence is someone like me." *Serkejh, 12*

◆ "Intelligence is something that can think for itself." *David, 11*

◆ "I think it means being smart and thinking of new ways to do things." *Amy, 10*

◆ "Being able to strengthen your brain." *Dave, 10*

◆ "Being a good thinker with a creative imagination."
Elizabeth, 10

◆ "Intelligence is not just knowledge, but being able to draw new conclusions and theories/ideas from your knowledge." *Andrea, 12*

◆ "Intelligence is thinking hard." *Kenny, 9*

◆ "All people have intelligence. It just depends on how you use it." *Jessi, 9*

◆ "Intelligence is when you're aggressive at everything you do." *Jill, 11*

◆ "Using your intelligence means you try to be creative and inventive." *Nancy, 16*

◆ "I think intelligence is the ability to understand and be imaginative." *Julie, 12*

◆ "Intelligence is the ability to use what you have upstairs." *Justin, 13*

◆ "You can never say no to intelligence." *Kate, 9*

How would *you* define intelligence?

■ ■ ■ ■ ■ ■ ■ ■ ■ ■ ■ ■ ■ ■ ■ ■

MEASURING INTELLIGENCE

Years ago, someone squeaked out of having to provide a useful definition of intelligence by saying, "Intelligence is what intelligence tests measure." But what do intelligence tests test *for?* And how can we be certain that the tests are accurate if we're not even sure what intelligence *is?*

For many years, our society has been more concerned with measuring intelligence than defining it. Let's look at how the whole thing got started...and some of the arguments that have resulted.

The Intelligence Testers

★ Sir Frances Galton

About 110 years ago, Sir Frances Galton (he was one of Charles Darwin's cousins) began to study human intelligence. He thought that intelligence was something you inherited, like blue eyes or Type O blood, and that the amount of intelligence you were born with stayed the same until you died. Today we know that this is all baloney.

★ Alfred Binet

Binet, a French psychologist, is considered "the father of intelligence testing." In 1905, he and a colleague, Theodore Simon, made up a test that was supposed to show which students would succeed in school and which wouldn't. It was called the "Binet-Simon Scale."

The two men wanted to know things like, "Is a smart eight-year-old as smart as a nine- or ten-year-old?" So they designed activities and questions for specific age groups. Their goal was to find out what the "average" child of each age group could do. They determined a child's "mental age," or MA, by the type of tests the child was able to pass. If a six-year-old was able to pass the tests meant for eight-year-olds, then they assigned the six-year-old an MA of 8.

But other psychologists discovered problems with the Binet-Simon scale. Some 16-year-olds scored the same as ten-year-olds—and so did some five-year-olds. A better, more accurate kind of test was needed.

★ Wilhelm Stern

In 1912, building on what Binet and Simon and other researchers had done, Wilhelm Stern developed a mathematical equation that could be used to measure a person's "mental quotient." Later on, this became known as "intelligence quotient"—I.Q.

Here's how it works: Let's say an eight-year-old child passes all the tests meant for ten-year-olds. The child is assigned an MA of 10. Next, the MA is divided by the child's chronological age—8. Finally, the quotient is then multiplied by 100 to get the child's I.Q. score—in this case, 125.

$$10/8 \times 100 = 125$$

Because most people tested in this way were found to have mental ages very close to their chronological ages, they ended up with I.Q. scores of around 100. So 100 was considered to be the "average" I.Q. for any age.

The I.Q. test proved to be very popular. Millions of people were tested. About half of them were found to be of "average" intelligence, with I.Q.'s between 90 and 110. One-fourth were found to be of "below average" intelligence, with I.Q.'s between 60 and 90. And the remaining one-fourth were found to be of "above average" intelligence, with I.Q.'s between 110 and 150. These findings fit neatly into a bell-shaped curve, like this:

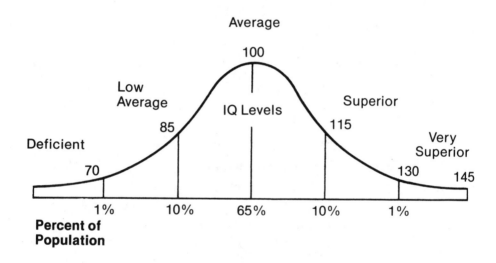

A lot of experts disagreed with what this graph seemed to say (and a lot still do). They argued that you can't measure a person's intelligence this easily, and that the whole concept of mental age is misleading because it implies that two people with the same mental age have the same type of mind.

Estimated I.Q.'s
of Celebrated People

I.Q. tests were all the rage in the early 1900's. In fact, it got so bad that people who had been dead for years (even centuries) were assigned I.Q. scores.

In 1926, for example, a group of psychologists published a study of the most eminent men who had lived between 1450 and 1850. Here are some of them and their *estimated* I.Q.'s:

		I.Q.
◆	John Stuart Mill, English writer and economist	190
◆	Johann Wolfgang von Goethe, German poet	185
◆	Voltaire, French writer	170
◆	Wolfgang Amadeus Mozart, Austrian composer	150
◆	Thomas Jefferson, third U.S. President	145
◆	Benjamin Franklin, U.S. diplomat, statesman, and scientist	145
◆	Charles Dickens, English novelist	145
◆	Leonardo da Vinci, Italian painter, scientist, and engineer	135
◆	Sir Isaac Newton, English mathematician	130
◆	George Washington, first U.S. President	125
◆	Johann Sebastian Bach, German composer	125
◆	Rembrandt van Rijn, Dutch painter	110

★ Lewis Terman

In 1916, Lewis Terman, a psychologist at Stanford University in California, took the ideas of Binet and Simon further and developed something called the *Stanford-Binet* test. Today this is the most widely used of all the intelligence tests.

The Stanford-Binet has been revised several times. It includes over 100 subtests and tasks. This may seem like a lot, but each one is quite short: it only takes 60-90 minutes to complete the entire test. How many subtests and tasks a person is asked to do depends on how old he or she is.

The Stanford-Binet has been widely used for nearly 70 years. Many people like it—and many people don't. Some think it puts too much emphasis on verbal and rote memory. Others think that a single score (which is all you get) can't possibly represent all of the complex thinking functions. Still others point out that the test doesn't measure creativity and isn't suitable for adults. In spite of such criticism, the Stanford-Binet is believed to be a good way of measuring "general intelligence."

★ David Wechsler

Some of the newest intelligence tests were designed by psychologist David Wechsler in the 1930's, 40's, and 50's. Today they are in use all over the country.

Wechsler felt that finding out a person's mental age wasn't enough to determine his or her I.Q. So he used mental age "equivalents" as guides, not as the final word. The first Wechsler Intelligence Scale for Children (WISC) was published in 1949. The revised version (WISC-R) came out in 1974 and has proved to be very popular.

Intelligence Tests vs. Achievement Tests

If you've been wearing your thinking cap while you've been reading this, you may have been wondering, "What's the difference between an *intelligence* test and an *achievement* test?"

Well, both kinds measure aptitude, learning, and achievement to some degree. But an intelligence test does more. It taps into a wider range of life experiences and looks for whether you apply what you know in new and different ways.

For example, when you take an intelligence test, you usually work with designs and pictures. Some psychologists believe that being able to mentally manipulate symbols is an important clue to intelligence levels. But what about the other clues? How can they be measured? Some intelligence tests may help predict what you are good at or what your *potential* is in a particular area.

An achievement test, on the other hand, tries to discover the facts you've learned at home and at school. (You probably remember filling in those little dots each fall or spring when it came time to measure how much you had learned.) An achievement test doesn't measure how you think or what your potential is. Either you know the answers, or you don't. Reading and math tests are both examples of achievement tests.

Which kind of test would *you* rather take?

The Trouble with Intelligence Tests

There does seem to be some connection between a person's I.Q. and how "smart" he or she is. For example, psychologists have found that people with higher I.Q.'s can process information and come up with responses more quickly than people with lower I.Q.'s.

Scientists have based countless conclusions on the results of intelligence tests. And educators have used these results in making decisions about students. *But the tests aren't perfect.* In fact, there's a lot wrong with them.

Maybe you've taken a group intelligence test in school. Instead of an I.Q. score, you received a percentile score. Maybe you and your parents and your teachers believed that this score told all about you and your brain. Unfortunately, your score may have been influenced by things *outside* your head—things you had no control over. Here are just a few examples:

??? Did someone read the test directions aloud? The *way* that person read the directions (emphasizing some words over others, maybe even getting some wrong) may have affected your score and the scores of everyone around you.

??? Was the test multiple choice? Did you guess at some of the answers? Guessing isn't a very good indicator of what you really know.

??? What if you're a super-creative person who finds more than one answer for a question? You could be penalized for this.

??? Is English your second language? Are you just learning English? How well a person does on an intelligence test often depends on how well he or she speaks the language of the test. Is this fair?

??? You probably took a *standardized* test. Standardized means that the test must first be tried out on groups of subjects from different age, income, and intelligence levels. But this trying-out process takes time...sometimes years. So your test may have been outdated.

Can any paper-and-pencil test measure *all* of your brain-related abilities? What if you're a terrific singer? What if you like to experiment with materials or invent new products? What if you can write beautiful poetry? What if you stole the show in the last class play? These kinds of things never show up on intelligence tests.

The controversy continues. Do the tests contain too much cultural bias? How do they account for genetic and environmental differences? Are they socially and racially fair, or do they favor a particular group? Which of the 200 tests available is the *best* one?

If these tests have so many problems, why do people keep taking (and giving) them? For one reason, old habits die hard. Our schools are used to testing. They think that test scores can predict a student's future success—even though this has never been proved! Still, colleges base admissions decisions at least partly on student test scores. And some employers refer to them when making hiring decisions.

There is one thing these tests are good for: predicting how well a person will do on later tests. That's because taking an intelligence test is like a game. The more times you play it, the better you get, and the more little tricks you learn.

Okay, maybe there's one more thing tests are good for: Many educators use them for diagnostic purposes. The tests point out students' strengths and weaknesses, and teachers can then teach to those strengths and weaknesses.

But what do intelligence tests do for *you*? Not much, as it turns out. An I.Q. score (or a percentile score) doesn't even scratch the surface of your capabilities. You have too many talents that don't relate to it. (Like baseball, singing, acting, inventing, and writing.) No intelligence test can begin to show how sensitive, creative, likable, or happy you are. It won't measure how eager you are to learn.

In other words, if you *do* take an I.Q. test, *don't take the results that seriously.* And don't bother to cram ahead of time with any of the hundreds of books on the market which promise to "raise" your I.Q. There's no secret formula or technique that can do that.

What if you do practice and end up with a higher score? Big deal. That won't make you any smarter. Besides, *it's not important.* What *is* important is to keep on learning, every day for the rest of your life—just because you can.

"The best way to find out if you can achieve something is to try to achieve it."

Arthur Jensen, who must not have been thinking when he said this; he was a famous scholar of heredity who believed that intelligence depended on genes

▲▲▲▲▲▲▲▲▲▲▲▲▲▲▲▲▲▲▲▲

If you want to know more about intelligence testing, read:

** *The Mismeasure of Man* by Stephen Jay Gould (New York: W.W. Norton and Company, 1981).

** *Straight Talk about Mental Tests* by Arthur R. Jensen (New York: The Free Press, 1981).

▼▼▼▼▼▼▼▼▼▼▼▼▼▼▼▼▼▼▼▼

NATURE VS. NURTURE

Have you ever wondered where your intelligence comes from? Has it been passed down to you in the genes you inherited from your parents? Or is it a result of your environment—the things and people, influences and stimuli around you?

Although scientists and scholars have been asking these questions for years, nobody has yet come up with *the* answer. That's why this issue is called the "nature vs. nurture controversy."

One thing we can't change are the genes and chromosomes we're born with. You inherited your genes from your parents, who got their genes from *their* parents, who got their genes from *their* parents, and on and on, back through time. It's easy to understand that we inherit ways of being smart. But does heredity determine how intelligent we are? Or is the brain a "blank slate" at birth, and do our experiences fill up that slate? You can see why this is called a controversy.

What We Know (Or Think We Know) So Far

- ◑ Your physical, mental, and emotional characteristics are a result of both your heredity and your environment.

- ◑ No two people have exactly the same genes (not even identical twins).

- ◑ No two people have exactly the same environment. (Remember that environment involves all sorts of things, including the way people interact. Even siblings raised in the same family will be treated differently by their parents, have different experiences at home and at school, and so on.)

- ◑ No two people perceive and respond to their environment in exactly the same way.

- ◑ What a person becomes, and the abilities he or she develops, often depend on how strongly genes and environment *complement* each other.

Studies of identical twins who have been separated at birth and raised in different homes and cultures have revealed important clues into this mystery. For example, researchers have learned that the skills and intelligence levels of twins raised apart from each other are very similar. So maybe heredity plays a larger role than we thought.

Can we draw any conclusions from what we've learned about the nature vs. nurture controversy? The most obvious is: We still have a *lot* to learn about where intelligence comes from. The most encouraging is: What you do with what you have is up to you.

Can You Teach an Old Rat New Tricks?

That's the question researchers in California have been trying to answer. Not surprisingly, they have found that an enriched environment can actually *increase* the number of connections between brain cells.

Dr. Marian Diamond, the scientist who found Einstein's frozen brain, did research with older rats. The group of rats who were treated to enriched environments grew more brain cell connectors. Dr. Diamond has concluded that our brains are like elastic. They "stretch" and get larger as they encounter new challenges.

If stimulation *helps* your brain, does lack of stimulation *hurt* your brain? Decide for yourself. Think about the last time you spent long hours watching dumb TV shows. Afterward, how did your brain feel? Dead or alive? Flabby or fit? Now that you know about Dr. Diamond's research, what are you going to do to stimulate your brain?

MULTIPLE INTELLIGENCES

The nature vs. nurture controversy has been raging for quite a while, and there's no sign that it will let up anytime soon. But that's not the only thing brain experts are arguing about.

Thanks to the brain, people are coming up with new ideas about intelligence all the time. One of the most fascinating is the notion of *multiple intelligences*. Two of the best-known names associated with this most recent debate are Yale psychologist Robert Sternberg (you read about him earlier, on pages 24–25), and Harvard psychologist Howard Gardner. Let's find out what each has to say.

Sternberg's Three Intelligences

Robert Sternberg believes that real life is where intelligence is at. He sees intelligence as a mental activity, or process, that people can be taught. In other words, he doesn't view intelligence as a built-in thing that you either have or you don't.

In his book, *Beyond I.Q.: A Triarchic Theory of Human Intelligence,* Sternberg defines three types of intelligence.

1. **Contextual intelligence** is the intelligence you use when you adapt to your environment, change your environment, or select a different environment to suit your needs.

2. **Experiential intelligence** is the intelligence you use whenever you build on your experience to solve problems in new situations.

3. **Internal intelligence** is the intelligence you use to approach a problem and evaluate the feedback to determine whether you should change your approach.

Sternberg has coined another term—"tacit knowledge"—to refer to "the things you need to know to succeed, but which are not necessarily taught or verbalized." For example, you call on your tacit knowledge when you're planning how to best use your time or resources. This is a kind of knowledge that you have to pick up on your own.

According to Sternberg, intelligence can be enhanced. Like many of his colleagues, he's convinced that we don't even come close to our true potential. But as more and more people start believing that they *can* succeed, it's very likely that they *will* succeed.

Gardner's Eight Intelligences

Howard Gardner approaches the issue of multiple intelligences from another perspective. He thinks that it's too limiting to focus on the mind alone, and that we can find better ways to measure and educate the human intellect if we expand our overall definition of intelligence. Gardner also believes that we should try to identify our most competent intelligence when we are younger (like your age) so we can continue to seek new knowledge.

In his book, *Intelligence Reframed: Multiple Intelligences for the 21st Century,* Gardner lists eight different kinds of human intelligence.

1. Linguistic intelligence enables you to write, listen and speak. It means choosing the right words and being sensitive to the many ways in which language is used. Poets, novelists, and public speakers have lots of linguistic intelligence.

2. Musical intelligence is the earliest to emerge. (Think of musical prodigies like Mozart, who began his career as a performer and composer at age 3.) It means being able to "hear" music and make sense out of pitch, rhythm, and musical sequences. Composers, musicians, singers, and dancers rely on their musical intelligence—and they all may use it in different ways.

3. Logical-mathematical intelligence makes it possible for you to put objects in some kind of order and to comprehend quantities. When you were younger, you used to do this mainly with physical objects (like blocks), but now you can probably do it in your head, too. Mathematicians and scientists display this intelligence when they go through long "chains" of reasoning.

4. Spatial intelligence enables you to perceive a form or an object, see the world accurately, and mentally "rotate" complex forms and imagine how they'll look when you turn them around. Visual perception and the ability to draw are part of it. Sculptors, inventors, engineers, painters, and chess players have high spatial intelligence.

5. **Bodily-kinesthetic intelligence** is what makes you good at handling objects or controlling your physical movements. Dancers, mime artists, swimmers, actors, and ball players have plenty of this intelligence.

6. **Intrapersonal intelligence** helps you to understand yourself and others. You use this intelligence to "key in" to other people's moods, temperaments, and intentions. This intelligence is the specialty of counselors, psychologists, and teachers.

7. **Interpersonal intelligence** enables you to notice other people's feelings and to make distinctions between them. Religious leaders, political leaders, and diplomats exhibit their strengths in this area.

8. **Naturalist intelligence** is what you use to observe, identify, and classify various things in nature or in your surroundings. You use it to examine and understand different kinds of plants, animals, or natural phenomena like clouds, stars, or rocks. Zoologists, forest rangers, farmers, veterinarians, and ecologists all use the naturalist intelligence in their work.

Gardner believes that all eight intelligences function independently but can be closely related. He also believes that when one or two intelligences are especially strong, they can "lead" a person in a certain direction. What are your talents? Which of the eight intelligences can you attribute them to?

Plus Gardner believes that each intelligence has its own "life history." An intelligence may "bloom" briefly and then fade away. But what if we could learn to hold onto all of our intelligences? What if we could learn to improve on the ones we're weak at? What if we could find a way to tap into different ones at different times?

TWO BRAINS ARE BETTER THAN ONE

Many parts of our bodies come in pairs: eyes, ears, hands, arms, legs, feet, brain.... That's right, *brain*. You have a pair of brains: a right side, and a left side. The two sides are called *hemispheres*, and they are connected by a thick bundle of nerves called the *corpus callosum*.

Actually, this connecting bundle of nerves is a communications network which relays information between the two hemispheres. Today we know that the corpus callosum carries about 4 billion messages per second.

The corpus callosum has been very important in helping us to understand the functions of each side. For years, neurosurgeons have been carefully studying people whose brains were injured in accidents or seizures. If a particular area was damaged, a person would not be able to talk or move his or her right arm or leg or other parts of the body. By examining these patients, doctors attempted to learn what parts of the brain were responsible for specific mental work and functions. This was a giant step in brain research, but it still left us with only a few rough guesses and many unanswered questions, simply because the brain is so complicated.

Remember that no two brains are alike or function in the same way. Our brains are as individual as our thumb prints. This is another reason why studying the two hemispheres can lead to confusion. And, to top it off, doctors have discovered that some areas of the brain switch jobs to handle new information.

What the Two Sides Do

As you may already know, the *left* hemisphere of the brain controls the *right* side of the body, while the *right* hemisphere of the brain controls the *left* side of the body. The reason for this is simple: The nerve fibers cross in either the spinal cord or the brain.

In most cases (but not all), the left hemisphere also controls these functions:

- ✔ **Language** (speech, facts, names, dates)
- ✔ **Sequential thinking** (processing information one step at a time)
- ✔ **Literal thinking** (understanding the literal meanings of words)
- ✔ **Logical thinking**
- ✔ **Mathematical thinking** (numbers and their relationships)
- ✔ **Reasoning**
- ✔ **Analysis**.

So your left brain generally takes care of reading, writing, and talking—your verbal skills. If it wasn't doing its job, you wouldn't be reading this page.

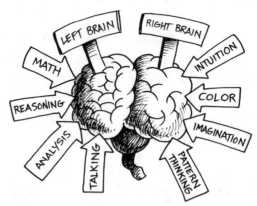

What about the right hemisphere? In most cases (but not all), it controls these functions:

- ✔ **Simultaneous processing** (processing different kinds of information at the same time and seeing the "big picture")
- ✔ **Imagination** (fantasies, dreams, daydreams)
- ✔ **Sense of color** (distinguishing colors, artistic abilities)
- ✔ **Musical abilities** (awareness of rhythms and emotions)
- ✔ **Pattern thinking** (ability to see patterns and relationships)
- ✔ **Spatial tasks**
- ✔ **Intuition**
- ✔ **Metaphorical thinking** (difference between what is said and what's meant).

So you might consider your right brain more "creative" or emotional. But be careful—most of the time, our left and right brains work together, sharing responsibilities and integrating streams of thought. Here are some examples of how they cooperate:

◆ When you sing a song, the right hemisphere maintains a sense of melody and rhythm while the left supplies the words and operates your vocal apparatus.

◆▷ When you write a description of a work of art, you begin by looking at it (right brain). But as soon as you start to write about it, the left brain takes over.

◆▷ When you solve a problem, the left brain does the deductive reasoning while the right brain contributes intuition and insight.

Throughout history, many significant creative discoveries have been made by people who used *both* sides of their brains.

◆▷ Leonardo da Vinci not only excelled in math, language, logical thinking, and analytical thinking; he was also great at using imagination, color, rhythm, and form.

◆▷ Albert Einstein discovered his Theory of Relativity by fantasizing what it would be like to ride a beam of light into space. Ideas came to him as pictures and images, and then he put them into words. (He once said, "My gift of fantasy has meant more to me than my talent for absorbing positive knowledge.")

◆ Charles Schulz, creator of Charlie Brown, Snoopy, Lucy, Linus, and the rest of the *Peanuts* gang, uses drawing to express almost any thought on any subject. A keen observer, he continually "draws" with his eyes.

◆ Steve Allen uses free association and dreams to create his books, songs, and albums. According to him, "a dream is like 827 moments of creativity all scotch-taped together."

◆ Laura Ingalls Wilder combined her language skills with metaphorical thinking and intuition to write books about her life as a pioneer girl. Starting with *Little House in the Big Woods*, each of her books is filled with the sights, sounds, and scents of pioneer America. Her philosophy was simple: "The true way to live is to enjoy every moment as it passes, and surely it is in the everyday things around us that the beauty of life lies."

Is It Unlucky to Be a Lefty?

The Latin word for "left" is *sinister*, which means "threatening" or "menacing" in English. Does that mean it's unlucky to be left-handed? Not at all. Being a lefty might be considered different, but different doesn't equal bad. In fact, lefties may be *better* at some things than right-handed people.

Here's just some of what researchers have learned:

👊 Lefties are better at designing in 3-D.

👊 Lefties are better at math.

👊 Lefties are better at remembering things.

 Lefties have a better chance of recovering from strokes or brain damage.

 Lefties are more likely to become artists, architects, musicians, engineers, or athletes.

So if you're a lefty, don't let it bother you. Just be comfortable with who you are.

If you want to know more about left-brain/right-brain theories and findings, read:

** *Drawing on the Right Side of the Brain* by Betty Edwards, revised edition (Los Angeles: J.P. Tarcher, Inc. 1989).

*** *Left Brain, Right Brain* by Sally P. Springer and George Deutsch, third edition (San Francisco: W.H. Freeman and Company, 1989).

SEX AND THE BRAIN

It's time to ask the question everyone has been waiting for: "Who's smarter, boys or girls?" In other words, are there any differences between the female brain and the male brain? If so, what are they?

It used to be that psychologists hesitated to investigate these issues because they didn't want to upset anyone. The mere thought that one sex might be "superior" to the other made people mad. But we can't escape the fact that there *are* differences between the sexes. Once we accept that, we can go on to explore them and add to our knowledge.

Exploring the Differences

We know that, on average, male brains weigh slightly more than female brains. However, the brain's weight as a percentage of total body weight is about the same for both sexes. We also know that males show more variability in intelligence than females. This means that there are more males than females with very high I.Q.'s—and more males than females with very *low* I.Q.'s. And while there are more male than female geniuses in the arts and sciences, there are also more males with mental disorders.

Why? Nobody knows for sure, but it could have something to do with the fact that in males, the two hemispheres of the brain seem more specialized than they are in females. Infant girls are born with a more highly developed cortex and a larger corpus callosum. Their right and left hemispheres are more closely inter-connected. Later in life, females tend to solve problems using several different approaches, while males seem more single-minded.

Dr. Jerry Levy, a well-known researcher from the University of Chicago, theorizes that the stronger corpus callosum link in the female brain could explain "women's intuition." It could also explain men's "superiority" in math and mechanical skills.

Some researchers have speculated that the structure of the male brain makes boys and men better at spatial tasks, like stacking colored blocks or putting things together. Dr. Julian Stanley of Johns Hopkins University thinks that this may be why males show stronger math-ematics ability than females. But there are females who have *excellent* spatial ability and males who have *poor* spa-tial ability. And there are female math whizzes and mechanics. So keep in mind that these differences don't describe the way *every* girl and boy acts.

Some researchers suggest that males have more highly developed motor skills and are better than females at solving problems involving the manipulation of objects (like jigsaw puzzles). Boys seem to be more interested than girls in how things work, and they gener-ally display more curiosity. They're also more impulsive and more easily distracted. They take more risks, and they're more aggressive.

Females appear to have more highly developed language skills and are better than males at controlling the fine hand movements needed for tasks like penmanship. They're less easily distracted, and they generally process information faster than males. Girls tend to be more interested than boys in people and social relationships, and they have an easier time remembering names and faces. Many girls have a stronger sense of odor, taste, and touch.

Physiology or Environment?

Now for the million-dollar question: Which of these differences are physiological, and which are due to environmental influences? Scientists emphasize that only *part* of the male-female difference in any one skill area is due to the anatomical and chemical makeup of the brain.

The other part—as much as 80 percent—depends on the person's level of expectation, the degree to which he or she is encouraged, and the style and extent of his or her education. In other words: Do you believe you can learn a specific skill? Do the people around you believe you can learn it? Are you given opportunities to learn it from excellent teachers? If you can answer "yes" to all three questions, then your chances of learning the skill are very high, even if your brain is "against" you!

Does this sound familiar? That's right: We're back with our old friend, the nature vs. nurture controversy. Many people today believe that a lot of these male-female differences might disappear if boys and girls were treated the same by their parents from the beginning. Society's expectations and our cultural values can affect how we learn and what we learn from the people around us.

Studies have shown that many girls are taught to be passive and nurturing, while many boys are taught to be independent risk-takers. Often without realizing it, parents encourage these tendencies by the types of clothing and toys they provide and the activities they allow their children to participate in. Later in life, boys are encouraged to do well in school while girls learn that it isn't "ladylike" to be smart.

Often, females end up in a no-win situation, afraid to fail *and* afraid to succeed. One interesting study found that when girls do fail, they tend to blame it on themselves or their intellectual inadequacies. But when boys fail, they say it's because they weren't motivated or didn't put forth the effort.

Why is it that girls are usually ahead of boys in grade school and start falling behind in high school? Why do females lack confidence and underestimate their abilities, while boys keep raising their expectations of themselves? Think about these questions. Then remind yourself that you deserve *every* possible chance to develop your abilities and be what *you* want to be.

66 66 66 66 66 66 66 66 66 66 66

"It doesn't take a little girl very long to look around and realize, 'There must be something wrong with me if I'm interested in math or science. I should be doing something else.'

"As a result, the country is losing an awful lot of extremely intelligent brainpower for the sciences, engineering, medicine, space program and other technical fields."

Dr. Sally Ride, a Ph.D. in physics and the first American woman astronaut in space

99 99 99 99 99 99 99 99 99 99 99

If you want to know more about male and female brain differences, read:

**   *Myths of Gender* by Ann Fausto-Sterling (New York: Basic Books, Inc., 1985).

**   *Smart Girls—Gifted Women* by Barbara A. Kerr, Ph.D. (Columbus: Ohio Psychology Publishing Company, 1987).

WHAT MAKES A PERSON A GENIUS?

In order to be called a "genius," a person usually has to accomplish something terrific. In other words, genius should not be equated with I.Q., although most geniuses do come from the high end of the I.Q. distribution.

If genius and I.Q. were the same, however, everyone with an I.Q. over 150 would be a genius. But there are plenty of high-I.Q. people sitting around doing nothing.

Nobody knows how and why some people become geniuses. But almost all geniuses have at least two things in common: They're *very* strongly motivated to achieve a goal or goals, and they feel secure and confident from childhood through adulthood.

Geniuses can be defined as people who have a knack for getting the most mileage out of their brains—people like Leonardo da Vinci, Mozart, Marie Curie, Thomas Edison, Margaret Mead, Steve Jobs, Walt Disney, Pablo Picasso, and Joe Montana. Most of the time, they're not even sure how they do it.

"Dumb Jocks" or Geniuses?

Since we've already learned that there are many sorts of intelligence, we should also realize that there are many ways to be a genius. For example, athletes are sometimes called "dumb jocks," but recent research by physicist and author Timothy Ferris reveals that some athletes may be the most intelligent humans on the planet.

Ferris believes that professional athletes like Joe Montana, quarterback for the San Francisco 49ers, exhibit their genius qualities by blending together a series of actions quickly and smoothly. Where does this unique skill originate? Ferris thinks that instructions are programmed into a part of the brain called the *premotor cortex* so athletes don't have to invent each motion in "real time."

In other words, Joe Montana is able to execute nearly every play without even thinking about it. As Montana himself once remarked, "If I ever stopped to think about what happens, what really makes things tick, after the ball hits my hand, it might screw up the whole process."

The premotor cortex also appears to be responsible for the achievements of artists such as cellist Yo-Yo Ma and dancer Twyla Tharp. Their ability to play or dance flows so smoothly it almost seems effortless.

Which do you think takes more brain power—playing center field for the Chicago Cubs, or teaching microbiology at Yale? Maybe the answer isn't a matter of amount, but of kind. And maybe jocks aren't "dumb" after all.

*"I believe that instinct is what makes
a genius a genius."*

Bob Dylan, American singer and songwriter

Child Prodigies and Other Achievers

You've probably read stories about "child geniuses" or "prodigies." These are the kids who can do word processing and compose poetry at age 3, read the encyclopedia at age 4, speak eight different languages by age 5, and/or start teaching math at a university at age 15. Incredible, but true.

What's the cause of their remarkable development? Scientists believe that it has something to do with being stimulated and encouraged at an early age. Apparently it's also related to the genes they inherit. But again, not *everybody* who grows up in an "enhanced" environment turns out to be a genius. Neither does *everybody* with great genes. Neither does *everybody* who has both.

Several years ago, Dr. Benjamin Bloom conducted a study to find out how 120 of the nation's top artists, athletes, and scholars had become so successful. He and his team of researchers learned that not all of their subjects had what could be called "natural talent." But they all *did* have drive and determination. For example, a famous concert pianist practiced several hours a day for 17 years to accomplish his goal, and an Olympic swimmer got up at 5:30 every morning to swim two hours before school started. Then she swam another two hours after school was over.

Plus these achievers all had *potential*. And that's something none of us lacks. No matter where we're born, where we live, or whose genes we inherit.

"We must believe that we are gifted for something, and that this thing, at whatever cost, must be obtained."

Marie Curie, Polish scientist and the first person to win
two Nobel prizes; along with her husband, Pierre,
she discovered radioactivity, which led to
radiation treatment for cancer

PROBLEM-SOLVING

Everyone has problems. And most kids have problems like these: "What should I wear today?" "How can I bring up my grade in this class?" "How can I earn more money?" "What can I write about for my term paper?" "What should I do on Saturday night?" "How can I get my little brother to stop bugging me?"

Luckily, you have what you need to solve almost every problem you'll encounter during your lifetime: your brain!

As you probably already know, successful problem-solving takes more than just gathering information. Sometimes you have to take a whole new approach—one you haven't tried before. Sometimes you have to stand back and try looking at the problem from different angles.

Think about how you would go about solving this problem:

The day before an important math test, your best friend tells you that her big brother gave her a copy of the test the teacher gave last year. She has already studied it and is willing to share it with you. You know that the test doesn't change much from one year to the next, and you're worried about passing, since math is your worst subject.

What will you tell your friend? And what will you do with the knowledge that your friend is cheating?

Naturally, it's easier to solve a made-up problem than to deal with the real thing. What was the last genuine problem *you* solved? How did you do it? What thinking processes did you use to arrive at a solution? Were you satisfied with the way you handled it? How would you do it if you could do it over?

Ten Terrific Tips for Making Life Easier

1. Don't assume that all problems are negative. Try to view some as opportunities to use your brain and take positive action.

2. Separate problems into categories. Which are related to goals in your life? Which are a result of being disorganized, or of not planning ahead?

3. Break problems down into as many elements as possible. Then break these elements down into steps. Then take each step one at a time.

4. Learn to distinguish *real* problems from *fantasy* problems—ones you've made up in your head. Maybe you're just imagining that a problem exists. Unnecessary worrying is a waste of brain power!

5. Work backwards. Don't focus only on the solution; the best one may not be obvious at the beginning. Instead, focus on the problem-solving process.

6. When faced with a particularly sticky problem, outline it on paper first. List the things you *want to do* about it. Then list the things you *can do* about it. Do the two lists match up?

7. Gather information. If any of your friends have dealt with similar problems, find out what they did. And don't hesitate to ask your parents for advice. As incredible as it seems, they used to be your age, and they may have lots of helpful suggestions.

8. Develop backup plans. If things don't turn out the way you want them to, what will you do then?

9. Be flexible in the way you approach problem-solving. Most of us develop problem-solving styles that turn into habits: We approach problems in the same old way, time after time. Maybe you need a change.

10. Don't be afraid to "talk to yourself." Some of the most successful problem-solvers think aloud.

▲ ▲ ▲ ▲ ▲ ▲ ▲ ▲ ▲ ▲ ▲ ▲ ▲ ▲ ▲ ▲ ▲ ▲

If you want to know more about problem-solving techniques, read:

* *The Ideal Problem Solver* by John D. Bransford and Barry S. Stein (New York: W.H. Freeman and Company, 1984).

* *A Whack on the Side of the Head* by Roger von Oech, Ph.D. (New York: Warner Books, 1990).

** *Universal Traveler: A Soft-System Guide to Creativity and Problem-Solving* by Don Koberg and Jim Bagnall (Los Altos, CA: William Kaufman, Inc., 1988).

▼ ▼ ▼ ▼ ▼ ▼ ▼ ▼ ▼ ▼ ▼ ▼ ▼ ▼ ▼ ▼ ▼ ▼

THOUGHTS ABOUT THINKING

$$3 + 4 = \boxed{?}$$

$$\square \, \bigcirc \, \triangle \, \square \, \bigcirc \, \triangle \, \square \quad \underline{?}$$

$$3, 6, 9, 12, \boxed{?}$$

Before you realized that these three lines were problems to be solved, you were already *thinking* about them. From birth (and maybe before), we humans are blessed with the fantastic ability to think. We do it constantly. Sometimes we're aware (conscious) of our mental activities, and other times we're unaware (unconscious) of them. Most thinking is automatic and takes place below the conscious level. It's a natural process, like breathing.

Consider some of the different kinds of thinking we do:

intuitive	lateral
logical	linear
conscious	subconscious
abstract	imaginative
evaluative	concrete
pattern	divergent
open-ended	sequential
convergent	metaphorical

A lot of these overlap. Even so, thinking about so many types of thinking can boggle the mind!

Now consider the fact that we can think in several ways and about several things at once. You can talk on the telephone and comb your hair...listen to the radio and do your homework...watch TV and work on a science project...read a book and eat lunch...doodle on your folder during a boring social studies lesson....

Thinking is a personal, private process. Because no two brains are exactly alike, no two people think exactly alike—even when they're in the same place doing the same things. Try this the next time you have a friend over: Get pencils and paper for both of you, sit down together at a table, and spend five minutes writing down whatever thoughts run through your heads. Then compare what you've written. You'll be amazed!

Some people are afraid to think. Some people are better thinkers than others. What a lot of people don't realize is that *thinking is a skill*. It can be wasted—or it can be improved. Let's look closely at some of the different kinds of thinking and how *you* can get better at them.

Imagination and Visualization

Thinking is more than just absorbing information. It involves a variety of mental activities. Most of these fit into the category of *imagination*.

Albert Einstein, one of the all-time champion thinkers, once said that "imagination is more important than knowledge." He valued his ability to visualize and create images. Many of his important discoveries and equations started there.

Imagination has been called "the essential tool of human intelligence." With it, we can invent new realities. We can form mental images of something without sensing it, and sometimes without ever having seen it before. We can make up characters and look into the future. We can bring the past back to life. There's no limit to what the imagination can do.

Imagined images aren't tied to any specific reference point. They can come from anywhere and lead anywhere you want them to. Your conscious mind is a storehouse of thousands of images. How can you tap into them? Sometimes the best way to do this is *not to try*. Just relax! Many people get their brightest ideas (the "AHAs!") while riding in a car, walking, bathing or showering, reading, listening to music, or dropping off to sleep. When do you get yours?

Imagined images don't always take the form of mental pictures. In fact, only one person out of four is capable of making good mental pictures. This doesn't mean that the other three people have poor imaginations. They may be able to imagine touches, sounds, body feelings, or abstract concepts instead.

To find out more about how your imagination works, try putting yourself inside these scenes:

- You're part of a team that's just climbed Mount Everest.
- You've been chosen to lead the next Space Shuttle launch.
- You're a famous rock star about to go on stage at Madison Square Garden.
- You're an Egyptian pharaoh living along the banks of the Nile River.

Can you "see" yourself in each situation? Describe your surroundings. What can you smell, taste, "feel"? What are you wearing? What's going on around you?

Your imagination may be all in your head, but its effects are often felt all through your body. To find out how, try these imaging exercises:

 You take a big, juicy lemon out of the refrigerator, cut it into quarters, bring one quarter toward your mouth...and sink your teeth into it.

 You sense the presence of something on your arm. You look down and see a big, creepy spider slowly making its way toward your shoulder.

 You're crouched in the open door of a plane, wearing a parachute. You're thousands of feet above the ground and the wind is howling around you. Someone gives you a shove—and out you go!

Did thinking about the lemon get your salivary glands going? Did thinking about the spider send shivers down your spine? Did thinking about jumping out of a plane cause your heart to beat faster or your breathing to accelerate?

Some people's imaginations roam most freely when they're most relaxed—flat on their backs and sound asleep. When we dream, our imagination takes center stage. We'll talk more about dreaming later. (If you can't wait, turn to pages 131–133.)

Logical Thinking

"I have track practice after school today. Guess I'll take my track shoes with me." Makes sense, right? So does most of the logical thinking we do. And we do so much of it during a normal day that we're hardly even aware of it.

Nobody knows exactly how logical thinking works, but it seems to be related to the ways in which we organize and associate ideas. It's believed to be a function of the left brain.

When we think logically, we begin with certain assumptions and concepts. Then we generate ideas, step by step, until we arrive at an "end point," or a solution. Much of this step-by-step thinking goes on below the conscious level.

For example, several distinct thoughts may take place in between "I have track practice after school today" and "Guess I'll take my track shoes with me." Some of these may include, "Track practice...running...feet on cinders...need to protect feet...need special shoes...track shoes...know where they are...get them out of closet and put them by door so I won't forget them tomorrow morning...." The conscious part of your brain "leaps" over these intermediate steps to reach a conclusion. And it happens very quickly—almost instantaneously.

Even though logical thinking often occurs naturally, without our being aware of it, we can get better at it. In fact, we *should* get better at it, for our own good. Every day, we're bombarded with tons of information from all directions: TV, radio, magazines, newspapers, school, conversations with parents and friends, and on and on. We need to know what's important, what's not, what we need, what we can do without, what to store, and what to ignore. If we didn't make these distinctions, our thinking would degenerate into nonsense. What if you thought, "I have track practice after school today. Guess I'll take my pet alligator with me"?

Actually, logical thinking is a pretty straightforward process. Most of the time, it involves making conclusions based on certain known facts. Here's a simple logical argument you're probably familiar with:

I. All A's are B's.

2. All B's are C's.

3. Therefore, all A's are C's.

But even with this simple three-step process, you have to be careful. If your facts aren't correct, it won't work. For example:

I. All basketball players are tall.

2. All tall people are funny.

3. Therefore, all basketball players are funny.

The trouble with this line of reasoning is that it isn't based on truths. *All* basketball players aren't tall (even though most of them are). And *all* tall people aren't funny (even though some of them are). So unless you're talking about the hilarious Harlem Globetrotters during a game, this argument is a loser!

Use this pattern to make up your own logical argument. But be careful with your facts.

I. All _____ are _____.

2. All _____ are _____.

3. Therefore, all _____ are _____.

Another type of logical argument goes like this:

I. All B's are C.

2. A is a C.

3. Therefore, A is a B.

For example:

I. All cars have four wheels.

2. A Chevrolet Camaro has four wheels.

3. Therefore, a Chevrolet Camaro is a car.

So far, so good. But what about this?

I. All cars have four wheels.

2. A skateboard has four wheels.

3. Therefore, a skateboard is a car.

The first argument is correct; the second is false. Can you see why?

Logical thinking involves making assumptions—but sometimes we can't assume too much!

One way to understand logical thinking is by looking at how *illogical* it can be. Here's another silly example:

I. I like caramel corn and green grapes.

2. I am a good student.

3. Therefore, anyone who doesn't like caramel corn and green grapes isn't a good student.

Some logical fallacies aren't easy to spot. It takes a keen observer to analyze a supposedly logical thinking process and discover the flaws. This, too, is something you can get better at—with practice. The next time you're watching a TV newscast or reading the newspaper, see if you can pick out an example of illogical thinking in the information being presented. You may be very surprised by what you discover.

How can you avoid crooked thinking? By checking your facts, avoiding unfounded assumptions, and paying attention to what you see and hear. Try not to get trapped by arguments that only *seem* logical.

Intuition

Intuition isn't a mysterious talent reserved for only a few special people. In fact, it's almost impossible *not* to be intuitive. The trick lies in being sensitive to what our intuition tells us—and knowing when it's steering us in the wrong direction.

How many times have you said, "I have a hunch that this is the right answer," or "I have a gut feeling about this"? How often have you sensed someone walking up behind you before you heard footsteps? How often have you known what someone else was thinking or feeling? In each case, your intuition was at work.

Where does intuition come from? Past experience, mostly. The things we've done or observed before collect in our minds until some situations seem "familiar" and we know what to expect from them.

Intuition has been called the "sixth sense." We can hear it and clearly understand it. It often speaks to us on a physical level. If we're about to be sick, our intuition helps us find ways to relieve our discomfort.

Athletes are always using their intuition. They don't have time to think about every move or play, so they rely on their subconscious to tell them what to do. (Remember what you read about Joe Montana on page 56?)

How much should *you* trust *your* intuition? That's the same as asking how much you should trust your logical thinking. Either one can fool you. Often, the two types of thinking work best when they're used together. Start by carefully studying a situation, then let your intuition guide you toward your final conclusion or decision.

How can you improve your intuitive powers? No one really knows, since intuition doesn't seem to be something you can practice. But people who are especially intuitive share certain characteristics, like patience, humility, self-control, and the ability to relax.

Incidentally, intuition doesn't seem to be related to a person's sex, no matter how much you may have heard about "women's intuition." Lots of males are intuitive, too.

Daydreaming

In the middle of math class, you relive the basketball game you went to last weekend. While washing dishes after dinner, you picture the new compact disc player you're saving up to buy.

Daydreaming! It's that marvelous ability to take a mind-trip away from where we are to someplace we'd rather be.

Daydreaming is a special kind of thinking. It combines memory, imagination, and intuition. Like the dreams we have while we're asleep, a daydream may involve scenes, objects, and people we know and don't know. The difference between daydreams and night dreams is that we can control the former.

Almost everybody daydreams, but very few people know how to use this ability to their advantage. Daydreaming can help us solve problems and become more creative. Unfortunately, it's seldom welcome in school. Because students usually get scolded for not paying attention, many never discover that they can use their daydreams to generate new ideas.

It would be great if we could somehow convince our teachers and parents that daydreaming can be good for us. Any ideas?

Your daydreams are like movies, and you're the director. Studies have shown that about 96 percent of all people daydream at some time or another—about success, about failure, about going on adventures, about people they know or would like to know. As kids become more aware of the opposite sex, they tend to spend a lot of time on romantic daydreams. Your daydreams can take you wherever you want to go.

To improve your daydreaming skills, try setting aside a half-hour each day when there's nothing else you have to do. Get comfortable and turn your mind loose. Afterward, think about where your daydreaming led you.

Pattern Thinking

Ever since you were born, sensory stimuli have been tracing "patterns" in your brain tissue—almost like road maps. The messages you've received through your sight, hearing, touch, smelling, and tasting have been organized into patterns and stamped into your brain.

These mental patterns are useful—actually, *essential*—because they help you to recognize familiar objects or circumstances. You know what to do without having to stop and figure it out. We all rely on pattern thinking, even though we're usually unaware of it.

Pattern thinking is what tells you that a cat is a cat, not a camel. It's what helps you to recognize your parents, your friends, your teachers, your neighbors. It lets you know that a fork is for eating with, not scratching with. It teaches you to stop on red and go on green.

Pattern thinking can enhance the efficiency of all our perceptual processes, especially our visualization and organization skills. Unfortunately, it can also get us stuck in a rut. Once you get used to one pattern, it's hard to go beyond it.

Take a look at Figure 1. What do you see—faces or a vase? If you've never seen this picture before, you may have noticed both, shifting back and forth until you settled on one. But if you *have* seen this picture before, chances are you see the same thing now that you saw back then. It's hard to get beyond a pattern that you're used to.

You can force yourself to break or change a pattern. Try it right now by looking at the picture again. If you see faces, make yourself see a vase. If you see a vase, make yourself see faces. Remember: It's all in your head!

– FIGURE 1 –

Tricky Thinking

Did you ever think that your mind was playing tricks on you? Take a look at Figure 2. Which line is longer, A-B or C-D?

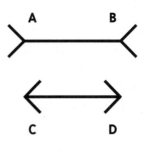

– FIGURE 2 –

Line A-B *looks* longer. But try measuring it with a ruler. Then measure line C-D. What do you discover?

Together, these lines create an *optical illusion*. An optical illusion is a trick for the eyes and the brain. You *think* you see something, but look again—and don't always believe everything you think you see.

Figure 3 is another optical illusion to challenge your mind and eyes. Where do the three prongs come from? When you follow them back to their source, what do you find? Try drawing this image on another sheet of paper. What happens?

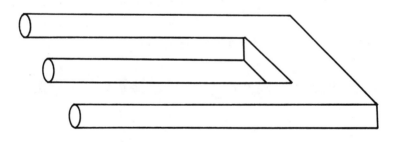

– FIGURE 3 –

How is it possible to make a mistake about something you're seeing? Because it's not just your eyes that help you to see. The neurons in your brain and the nerve cells in your eyes are key helpers. So you're also "seeing" the object with your brain, which is interpreting what you see.

You may not see the same illusions your friends see. That's because you have different previous experiences. Scientists have discovered that the people of certain African tribes can't see illusions that show objects in perspective or objects with right angles. They have never seen drawings or photographs of things in perspective, so the illusions don't make sense to them. They live in round houses, and their doors have curved edges, so right angles are not part of their previous experience.

Did you ever look at something quickly and then look at it again, and suddenly you "see" something else? That's because some illusions can "change" right before your eyes. Look at Figure 4. Do you see an old woman, or a young woman?

– FIGURE 4 –

Now look at Figure 5. Do you see a duck, or a rabbit?

– FIGURE 5 –

Optical illusions have fascinated and intrigued humans from as far back as prehistoric times; we know this from the cave drawings that prehistoric peoples left behind. Many painters and artists have used optical illusions to achieve certain effects. The illusions of modern artist M.C. Escher can really boggle your brain! Find some of his work and look carefully at the details. You'll be amazed at what your eyes (and brain) can see.

Most people enjoy optical illusions and think they're fun. But did you ever stop to think about how valuable and useful they could be? In nature, plants and animals use illusions to hide or disguise themselves. Camouflage saves lives during wartime. Optical illusions make movies and TV programs more interesting and fun to watch. Take a good look around you and find more examples of optical illusions at work.

Positive Thinking

Unless you've been a hermit for the past ten years, you've heard about the power of positive thinking. People who have it claim that it works miracles. And they may be right.

Positive thinking means making your brain work *for* you rather than *against* you. It involves seeing things positively and using positive words to express your thoughts and feelings. In a way, it's a form of self-hypnosis. And it's really very simple. Tell yourself that you're terrible at geometry, and you probably will be. But tell yourself that you're getting better at it every day and you will!

Positive thinking focuses on success. Positive thinkers don't program themselves *not to lose*; they program themselves *to win*. They don't program themselves *not to be dull*; they program themselves *to be alert*. There's a big difference.

Think of a class you'd like to do better in. Start telling yourself, every day, "This is an interesting class. I'm starting to like it more. I can do well here." Just saying these words will make you feel optimistic and more capable. Thinking positively can go a long way toward helping you achieve your goals.

If negative thoughts start creeping into your mind, try getting rid of them like this: Imagine yourself kicking them out. Put them into a mental picture of a creature you despise (like a monster—or a cockroach). This will arouse your feelings of aggression, and you'll be able to envision yourself giving the creature the boot.

Another way to increase your personal power of positive thinking is by cutting negative phrases out of your vocabulary. Like these:

"I hate..."   "I can't..."

"I'm sick of..."   "I'm afraid of..."

"That's impossible..." "That'll never work..."

"Everything I do turns out wrong..."

What other phrases do you use that belong on this list? Write them down on a piece of paper. Then tear it up and throw it away! Now write down positive phrases like these:

"I can do it..."   *"Let's give it a try..."*

"Why not?"   *"I think it'll work!"*

Add your own phrases to this list, and post it somewhere in your room where you'll be sure to see it every day.

Another technique to try is called "self-talk" or "inner speech." Self-talk is anything you say to yourself, in your mind or out loud. Think about the last time you forgot your homework at home. Or think about the last time you dropped something breakable on the floor. What did you say to yourself? Did you use words like "dumb," "failure," "lazy," "clumsy," "ugly," "stupid," "clod," "loser," "jerk," or "disorganized"? Eliminate them from your mental vocabulary, starting today.

It helps to have a "cheer-up" sentence in reserve for those times when you're really feeling down, depressed, defeated, or lonely. Here are a few examples to store in your mind:

"I'm healthy, strong, and comfortable."

"I'm good at _____, _____, and _____."

"The people who like me include _____, _____, and _____."

"The last really terrific thing I did was _____."

Remember: You are what you think you are.

Three Ways to Sharpen Your Thinking Skills

Thinking is something you're going to have to keep doing for the rest of your life. Here are a few ways to get better and better at it:

I. Learn to see the "big picture."

Some people can grasp bits and pieces of a situation but have a hard time viewing it as a whole. Seeing the "big picture" takes *strategic thinking,* and it's something you can practice.

Start by asking yourself this very simple question: "What's going on?" Then break it down into specifics, like this:

??? Where are you? Scan your setting and note details.

??? Who are you with? If there are other people present, pay attention to what they're doing.

??? What is your relationship to the people you're with? That may determine what you do next.

2. Learn to think on your feet.

There are people who are good at this. You know who they are—the ones who are always coming up with a snappy line or a split-second solution to a problem.

Start by closely observing your situation. Again, ask yourself: What's going on? Where are you? Who are you with? What are they doing? What's your relationship to them? Think about what *you* want. Set clear goals.

Don't procrastinate. Act! Maybe the decision you make won't be the best one possible. But at least you will have done something. And the better you get at thinking on your feet, the better your decisions will become.

3. Be flexible.

According to a study done at Colgate University, students who took math tests while lying on the floor with their feet slightly raised did better than students who sat upright at their desks. They finished the test 8 percent faster—and their answers were 14 percent more accurate. Maybe your teacher won't let you take math tests while lying on the floor. But it can't hurt to ask!

Here are more ideas to consider:

- Do you always do your homework before dinner? Try doing it later for a week or so. You may notice an improvement.

- Take notes on colored typing paper instead of lined white notebook sheets. The colors may inspire you.

- The next time you start a new class, don't head for your "usual" spot. Sit in the front or the middle. Sit by the door instead of by the window.

"The world is a tragedy to those who feel, and a comedy to those who think."

William Shakespeare, English playwright, poet, and actor, author of at least 37 comedies, histories, and tragedies, and knowledgeable in subjects including music, law, science, stage art, and sports

The Art of Listening

When you're supposed to be listening, do things go "in one ear and out the other?" That's an entertaining image, but it doesn't describe what actually happens. All kinds of sounds—talking, music, traffic noises, airplanes flying overhead, birds chirping, floorboards squeaking—come into your head through your ears every day. And they don't exit out the other side. Instead, your brain chooses to use them or lose them.

You have a lot of control over what you listen to. One reason is because your brain processes information four to ten times faster than the speed of speech. So even if you wanted to, you couldn't take it all in. But you can decide what to pay attention to and retain.

Remember the last time you sat through a particularly boring lecture? Did your mind wander off in a million different directions? Being a good listener involves more than keeping your ears open and your mouth closed. It's a perceptual skill that depends on your attitude. The next time you're about to tune out, ask yourself: "Am I willing to learn something new? Can I convince myself to get interested? Are there advantages to listening closely to what's being said? Can this information help me to reach a particular goal?"

Too many people have poor listening habits. They're so wrapped up in themselves and what they're going to say or do next that they neglect to listen. Or they're easily distracted. Or they seem to listen closely, but immediately forget everything they hear.

Many businesses and companies are training their employees to be better listeners. Schools should be doing the same with their students. Most aren't, and that's too bad, because students spend 60 to 70 percent of their classroom time listening. Or, at least, that's what they're *supposed* to be doing.

What kind of listener are you? Here are two ways to sharpen your listening skills:

 The next time you end up in a boring situation (and there will be a next time), don't tune out. Instead, tune in. Be "all ears" for a change and see what happens.

 Don't just sit there; *do something.* Take notes, placing special emphasis on key words or phrases. Make lists: of questions to ask afterward, of ideas to explore further on your own, of points you disagree with. Use these lists later on to refresh your memory.

▲▲▲▲▲▲▲▲▲▲▲▲▲▲▲▲▲▲

If you want to know more about thinking, read:

*   *The Optical Illusion Book* by Seymour Simon (New York: William Morrow and Company, 1984).

*   *Tricks of Eye and Mind* by Larry Kettelkamp (New York: William Morrow and Company, 1974).

**   *Brain Building* by Marilyn vos Savant (New York: Bantam Books, 1990).

**   *Learn to Improve Your Thinking Skills* by Karl Albrecht (Englewood Cliffs, NJ: Prentice-Hall, Inc., 1980).

**   *Make the Most of Your Mind* by Tony Buzan (New York: Linden Press/Simon and Schuster, 1984).

▼▼▼▼▼▼▼▼▼▼▼▼▼▼▼▼▼▼

MEMORY AND LEARNING

You stroll into class and sit down at your desk. Then your teacher gives you your first assignment of the day:

Memorize this list of numbers in less than one minute:

1518593765502157841665950611290485686772731418186105462974801294974965928.

Sounds impossible, right? But a young university student from Pittsburgh named Dario Donetelli was able to repeat this list (in order, with no mistakes) only *48 seconds* after hearing it.

Another person with an awesome memory was the Russian journalist Solomon Shereshevskii, known as "S." Although he never took notes, "S" could repeat everything that was ever said to him, word for word. (If someone sneezed, "S" would have trouble recalling what was said, because the sneeze was like a blur in his memory.)

"S" had such remarkable imagery and memory capacity that he ended up being a stage performer. Unfortunately, he was unable to forget anything and ended up with *too much* information packed inside his head. He became easily confused and couldn't even hold a normal conversation.

Most people don't have memories like Dario or "S," but our memories are amazing just the same. How many thoughts do you take in during a normal day? 50? 200? 5,000? 10,000? Maybe 50 seems too low and 10,000 seems too high. Surprise: You actually take in *billions* of thoughts within each 24-hour period.

Within the three pounds of wrinkled flesh that makes up your brain are telephone numbers, commercial jingles, the taste of yesterday's school lunch, faces of famous people, birthdays, the way a dog's coat feels, the smell of your grandma's perfume...all the images, facts, and experiences of a lifetime.

Your memory plays an important role in *everything* you do. All learning depends on memory—and memory is far more than simply recalling a lot of facts. It also involves remembering thinking patterns. (Like the logical thinking patterns you read about on pages 67–69.)

The human memory is powerful and mysterious. No two people remember exactly the same things in exactly the same ways, even if their lives are almost identical. No one knows exactly how memory works or why it fails us at times. That's because studying the memory is like trying to understand the workings of a complicated machine without being able to take it apart and look inside.

Memory seems to be located everywhere and nowhere in the brain. And your brain seems to have an unlimited capacity for storing memories. If you took in 1,000 new bits of information every second from the day you were born until you were very old, you'd still have plenty of room left over.

Our brain takes in more information than we realize. Some experts think that it may actually remember *everything* we hear, taste, smell, touch, see, and experience. Others disagree. They claim that if this happened, we'd be overloaded and maybe even schizophrenic.

How does your brain decide what to toss out and what to keep? You might think of your brain as a kind of sieve or filter. It sifts through the loads of information you take in and selects what to screen out. Otherwise, your brain would be jam-packed.

Over 2,000 years ago, the Greek philosopher Aristotle suggested that the mind was "imprinted" with memories—like soft wax imprinted with a ring. Scientists today are discovering that he may have been right.

In 1969, a Canadian professor named Wilde Penfield conducted a series of experiments on the brains of some of his patients. When he stimulated certain parts with small electrical charges, the patients were able to visualize mental pictures from the past—including long-buried memories from childhood. They also got impressions of sounds, smells, colors, and tastes related to these past events. Penfield's experiments seem to indicate that memory "pathways" or "traces" do exist.

It would take another whole book to begin to explain the many theories about how the brain stores information. For now, let's leave it at this: Whenever your senses take in any kind of data, electrochemical circuits are formed between your neurons. These "connections" are what result in stored memories.

Six Types of Memory

On pages 40–43, you read about the possibility that we might have many different intelligences. That issue is still open to question. Most scientists do agree, however, that we have several types of memory. Let's look at some of these.

1. **Short-term memory**, also called the "working memory," stores information you need for only a brief period of time. This type of memory includes the ability to recall from six to eight different items within specific categories. Examples: your spelling words for this week, the melodies to popular songs, license plate numbers. When you cram for a test, you're using your short-term memory.

2. **Long-term memory** stores information over a long period of time so you can get it when you need it. Examples: your best friend's telephone number, your father's birthday, the meanings of words, a foreign language.

3. **Sensory memory** is important to the way you perceive the world. It contains sensory impressions that you never forget, like the taste of peppermint candy, the sound of your favorite rock song, the smell of roses, and the way a cat's fur feels. Almost *every* taste or smell you experience forms a permanent record in your brain.

4. **Motor skill memory** has to do with physical activities like riding a bicycle, throwing a ball, brushing your teeth, and swimming. These are things you learn by repetition, which makes them very hard to forget. (Practice doesn't just make perfect; it also makes permanent!)

**"I hear and I forget;
I see and I remember;
I do and I understand."**

Old Oriental saying

5. **Verbal/semantic memory** enables you to know the meanings of words and math concepts. Most of us can remember several hundred thousand words and their meanings. Some of the things you've read about in this book have probably entered your verbal/semantic memory.

6. **Photographic memory**, also called "picture memory," stores images that remain as vivid as photographs in your mind. People who have a highly developed form of this type of memory can remember whole pages of books, including punctuation marks. Unfortunately, photographic memory usually lasts only for a short period of time.

A sort of "subcategory" of photographic memory is called *eidetic memory*, and it's fairly common in young children; about 20 out of every 500 kids have it. But it usually fades away before age 13. Maybe that's because our educational system stresses logic and language over imagination.

Déjà Vu: The Mind's Twilight Zone

Have you ever had the experience of being in an entirely new situation when suddenly you're *sure* you've lived through it before? Did it seem as if you *knew* your surroundings, the people around you, and the feelings you were having? This eerie experience is known as *déjà vu*. Scientists think that it may be related to something called "memory units." These memory units might be so complete that they include vivid and accurate sensory pictures of a place, setting, or circumstance.

Psychologist Carl Jung believed that we all have a "memory storehouse" that we share with others at different times and places without realizing it. He thought that people everywhere could tap into each other's storehouses. The next time you have that déjà vu feeling, think about this: Maybe those aren't your memories at all. Maybe they're somebody else's memories!

Why We Forget

Now that we know something about how we remember, let's find out why we forget.

To begin with, nobody on Earth has a "perfect" memory. Some people may have better memories than others, and some may have photographic memories, but even they can't remember *everything* they experience during their lives. (Or, at least, they can't *retrieve* each and every one of their memories.)

In fact, most of us forget more than 99 percent of the phone numbers we learn, and more than 90 percent of the names of the people we meet. That's nothing to brag about! We've all had the feeling that a particular memory was "on the tip of our tongue"—and no matter how hard we tried, we weren't able to get to it.

The reasons why people forget are almost as numerous as the ways they remember. Here are just a few:

 Some people have cluttered minds, plain and simple. They need to do some "brain cleaning"!

Your brain doesn't have to be like a messy drawer, stuffed with mismatched socks and underwear. One way to keep it neat and organized is by assigning mental "labels" to new information coming in.

 Some people forget things because they're poor listeners and don't pay attention.

You learned about listening on pages 80–81. Another way to sharpen your listening (and memory) skills is to softly repeat to yourself something you really want to remember.

 Some people forget things because they're too painful to remember.

On the other hand, there are some painful memories—like our most embarrassing moments—that never go away, even though we wish they would! It seems as though the brain has a "safety valve" that releases some memories we don't want to keep.

 Other "memory blocks"—things that help you *not* to remember—include stress, mental strain, and fear.

It's possible to break down some of these blocks, but don't press too hard. Forcing yourself to remember something could backfire and make you forget even more. This may explain "stage fright" and the horrible feeling of not remembering *anything* after studying too hard for a test.

"There isn't an idea I've ever had that I haven't put down on paper."

Isaac Asimov, science fiction writer, author of nearly 500 books on a variety of subjects

How to Improve Your Memory

The bad news is: There are some things you *will* forget, no matter how hard you try to remember them. The good news is: You *can* improve your memory. Visit any library or bookstore and find tons of ideas for expanding your memory capacity. Some of them may be worth trying; others may be a big waste of time. Only you can decide what works for you.

The best approach to take is a very basic one: Use your memory as often as possible! The more you use it, the better it will get.

■ ■ ■ ■ ■ ■ ■ ■ ■ ■ ■ ■ ■ ■ ■ ■

HOW KIDS MEMORIZE THINGS

We asked over 450 kids ages 8-16 to share their "tricks" for memorizing things. Here's a sampling of what they said:

◆ "I can remember things by their special features." *Kelly, 10*

◆ "I try to make up a tune for it." *Melodie, 11*

◆ "I associate them with other things that I already know." *Shawn, 14*

◆ "I use initials and rhyming songs." *Elizabeth, 10*

◆ "If I have to memorize something, I'll memorize a word out of each sentence. That helps me with the whole thing." *Cindy, 15*

◆ "I use anagrams sometimes." *Melissa, 15*

◆ "Divide it into parts, count them, number them, then say it over and over while counting." *Marianne, 10*

◆ "I read them right before bed, or practice them a lot." *Tony, 12*

◆ "I sort of say things in a rhythm." *Rudy, 11*

These are all *great* ideas. Maybe you have ideas of your own that work for you. It doesn't matter what you do, as long as it does the job!

■ ■ ■ ■ ■ ■ ■ ■ ■ ■ ■ ■ ■ ■ ■ ■

Most of us are taught to memorize things in school. (And a lot of us end up hating the things we have to memorize. Too often, they're poems—and that's why so many grownups don't like poetry. What a shame!) But we're not taught how to make the most of our memories. *Rote memory*—the kind that comes from repeating things over and over, often without paying any attention to what they mean—doesn't begin to tap our potential.

Here are a few tips for improving your memory:

If there's something you really want to remember, write it down. Then, even if you forget it, you'll be able to learn it again.

Keep a calendar handy. A pocket-sized one can be used for making notes and jotting down thoughts you have during the day.

Keep a note pad and pencil by your bed. Some of our greatest ideas come to us just as we're dropping off to sleep.

If you're reading something you want to remember, read it aloud to yourself. You can improve your learning and memory by as much as 40 percent by using this simple technique.

Don't stick to just one way of memorizing things. You may want to try one method for memorizing poems, and another for memorizing math formulas.

Interestingly, the time of day may affect how much you remember. Studies have shown that you remember more if you study right before you go to sleep. Also, people usually remember more of something if they learn it in the afternoon instead of the morning. But *your* best time to learn can be *anytime*. Your brain is *always* taking in new information.

Mnemonics

Mnemonics—pronounced "nem-AH-niks"—are special memory tricks that can help you to remember almost anything. Your teachers have probably already taught you some mnemonics. Here are two more for you to try.

▶ **Acronyms**

Acronyms are short phrases or initials that can help you remember a particular sequence of words.

▪ Would you like to remember all the colors of the spectrum—the ones you see in the rainbow—in the correct order? Say hello to "ROY G. BIV," whose name stands for **R**ed, **O**range, **Y**ellow, **G**reen, **B**lue, **I**ndigo, and **V**iolet.

▪ What about the Great Lakes? Try "HOMES"— for **H**uron, **O**ntario, **M**ichigan, **E**rie, and **S**uperior.

▪ Maybe you already know the nine planets, starting with the one closest to the sun. If not, this silly sentence will help: "My Very Excellent Mom Just Served Us Nine Pizzas." It stands for **M**ercury, **V**enus, **E**arth, **M**ars, **J**upiter, **S**aturn, **U**ranus, **N**eptune, and **P**luto.

Create an acronym of your own for the parts of the brain: the **B**rain **S**tem, the **C**erebellum, the **C**erebrum, and the **C**ortex.

"B_____ S_____ C_____ C_____ C_____."

▶ The LOCI Technique

To use the LOCI technique, you visualize a "path" and specific "landmarks" along that path. Anything you want to remember is linked to a landmark. For example, let's say you need to remember a list of ten items to take on a camping trip.

1. Start by imagining a path through your house or apartment.

2. Now make a list of ten landmarks. You might choose these:

Kitchen sink	Bathtub	Stove
Refrigerator	Toilet	Cupboard
Medicine cabinet	Bedroom closet	Bed
	Dresser drawer	

3. Next, make a list of the ten items you need to bring on your trip. They might include:

Toothbrush	Matches
Sleeping bag	Underwear
Lantern	Marshmallows
Pans	Guitar
Insect repellent	Crossword puzzle books

4. Finally, match up the two lists in a made-up "story." Let your imagination go! That's one of the fun parts of the LOCI technique. You can imagine anything you like, and it doesn't have to make sense. Study the example on page 94.

You can use the LOCI technique with almost any place and item. The wildest images are often the most powerful ones, and they tend to stick with you longer. When you use the LOCI technique, try to include these:

 **extra-bright colors**

**rhythm**

silly or absurd connections

movement

sense of touch, taste, smell, and hearing, as well as seeing

exaggeration

 **humor.**

For example:

VISUALIZE YOUR [toothbrush] FLOATING IN THE KITCHEN [sink]

WHAT COLOR IS IT? NOW IMAGINE THAT THE [refrigerator] DOOR

IS OPEN BECAUSE THE [shirt] IS STICKING OUT OF IT.

NEXT YOU OPEN THE CUPBOARD [door] AND SEE THE

LIT [light bulb]. THEN YOU TOUCH THE HOT [stove] AND BURN

YOUR HAND ON THE [pan]. GO TO THE [cabinet] AND

GRAB THE LARGE CAN OF [INSECT OFF]. IN THE [bathtub] IS

A [brush]. TO YOUR SURPRISE, THE [toilet] IS CLOGGED

WITH YOUR [cup]. PROCEED TO YOUR BEDROOM

[closet], OPEN THE DOOR AND THERE'S A GIANT

[marshmallow] WAITING TO GOBBLE YOU UP. INSIDE YOUR

[dresser] YOU FIND YOUR OLD [guitar] WITH ALL ITS [strings]

MISSING. FINALLY, YOU REACH YOUR [bed] AND FIND

A PILE OF [FAVE CROSS books] THAT YOUR SISTER HAS SCRIBBLED IN.

If you want to find out more about memory and learning, read:

**   *How to Improve Your Memory Power* by Alan S. Brown (Glenview, IL: Scott Foresman, 1989).

**   *The Ultimate Memory Book* by Robert Sandstrom (Granada Hills, CA: Stepping Stone Books, 1990).

**   *Use Your Perfect Memory* by Tony Buzan (New York: E.P. Dutton, 1984).

CREATIVITY

★ Galileo made his first important scientific observation at age 17.

★ Tracy Austin won the National Junior Tennis Tournament at age 10 and played at Wimbledon when she was 14 years old. At age 17, she was ranked first in the world in women's tennis.

★ Georg Friedrich Handel composed music at age 11.

★ Although she was stricken by a severe illness that left her deaf, blind, and mute at the age of 19 months, Helen Keller went on to graduate from Radcliffe College *cum laude*—with honors.

★ Carl Gauss, a famous mathematician, was doing research at age 15.

★ Concert singer Marian Anderson began her career at age 6, taught herself to play piano at age 8, and won prizes for singing at age 21. She was the first black singer to perform with the Metropolitan Opera.

It's no accident that many incredible discoveries and achievements have been made by people in their teens and early 20's. This is not to say that your creativity will decline as your age increases. But right now, at this very moment, your young and relatively uncluttered brain has more room than it will ever have for new and brilliant ideas. So this may be the best time ever to enhance your creativity.

The Importance of Play

As you get older, it becomes harder to let your imagination run free. Remember when you were five or six years old and you could turn things into anything you wanted to? The empty refrigerator box in the garage became Captain Hook's pirate ship or an underground tunnel. A paper-towel tube became a spy glass. It was all part of your normal, everyday play. Creativity and imagination are built on playful ideas.

For some reason, people lose their creative spirit as they get older, just like they lose their baby teeth. But what causes this to happen? Do we simply grow out of our playful selves? Or are we afraid that others will make fun of us if we continue to be playful? No one knows for sure why our creative spirit seems to slip slowly away. But we *do* know that we can hang onto it if we really want to.

Think of all the creative adults who are still full of playfulness, talent, and ideas—Robin Williams, Bill Cosby, Whoopi Goldberg, Penn and Teller....No doubt there were times when other people told them, "That won't work"..."What a waste of time"..."Who needs it?"..."What's that?"...and even the dreaded, mind-deadening "Grow up!"

Maybe you've heard these discouraging words. And maybe you've decided to take them with a grain of salt. You know that it's hard to get anywhere without taking risks. So don't be afraid to keep playing, imagining, and using your creativity. Share your talents with others. You *will* find people who appreciate them, and people who appreciate *you*.

You Are Creative

Everyone exercises his or her creativity in unique and personal ways. As you come up with novel ways to comb your hair, fix your breakfast, set the table, do your homework, write a story, or arrange your room, you're being creative. The special ways you walk, dress, talk, and act also demonstrate your creativity.

Most experts agree: *Every* person is creative. In other words, creativity isn't something you either have or you don't. It's more a matter of degree than ability. Some people are creative in big, obvious ways, while others are more subtle about it.

Creativity, like intelligence, is hard to define and difficult to measure. By the way, there are no proven connections between creativity and I.Q. Just because a person is a genius doesn't necessarily mean that he or she is creative. On the other hand, a person who thinks creatively isn't necessarily tops on the intelligence scale.

Your creativity depends on what *you* do with what's in *your* head.

"Our rewards come not from having brains, but in using them."

Gerard I. Nierenberg, author of
The Art of Creative Thinking

Creativity Tricks and Techniques

How do creative people come up with their ideas? Sometimes they do it in very unusual ways. Many creative people have been considered eccentric and even weird.

- When he was a young man, Beethoven often poured cold water over his head because he thought it would stimulate his brain.

- Whenever he sat down to write, Charles Dickens would turn his head to the north because he thought the magnetic forces of the Pole would help him to create.

- Rudyard Kipling only used black ink to write with.

- Johann Schiller, a poet and playwright, was stimulated by the odor of decomposing apples, so he always kept some in his desk.

- Elizabeth Bishop, a poet, ate Roquefort cheese before going to bed because she thought it would help her to have interesting dreams that might inspire her poetry.

You probably have a few strange habits and routines of your own. When you're getting ready to create something, what do you do? Sit in a special chair? Wear a particular item of clothing? Rub your lucky penny?

Creative thinking leads to creative results. When you're thinking creatively, you're searching for ideas and using your knowledge and experience to go off in new directions. Knowledge is essential to creative thinking. In fact, every new idea is a combination of two or more *known* ideas.

Creativity doesn't spring up by accident. It's a mental process, and like any other mental process, it takes practice to get good at it. An open mind and a sense of humor can help. So can going beyond the expected and seeking out unexplored possibilities.

Another way to boost your creativity is by exercising your brain. Stretch your thinking by tackling these problems:

I. What is 1/2 of 13? (Don't stop with the obvious answer. After spending some time on this problem, turn to page 114 for some possible solutions.)

2. Write several captions for this cartoon.

When you look at problems from different perspectives and don't accept the first answer that comes to mind, you're practicing creative problem-solving. Part of this mental process involves making connections and linking ideas together, just for the fun of it.

Since the beginning of time, people have used their creative thinking powers to come up with extraordinary ideas. You can, too.

The Four Stages of Creative Thinking

Although there's no single method for improving creativity that's 100 percent effective, there are some creative processes that seem to work better than others. One that works especially well was invented by G. Wallas in 1926.

According to Wallas, creative thinking occurs in four major stages:

1. **Preparation** involves collecting knowledge and information for the problem under consideration. (Before he could create his sculptures, Michelangelo had to learn about human anatomy.)

2. **Incubation** involves resting and relaxing to allow images from the unconscious to surface. During this "sitting and thinking" time, the creative thinker starts visualizing parts of the idea or solution. (Einstein once told a friend that he got some of his best ideas while shaving.)

3. **Illumination** comes suddenly and unexpectedly. The idea or solution just pops into your brain. The light bulb goes off over your head and you experience an "AHA!" (Isaac Newton got his first insight into gravity while sitting in an apple orchard and watching an apple fall from a tree.)

4. **Verification** involves testing, proving, and carrying out an idea or solution to see if it really works. (The Wright Brothers tested their biplane by keeping it in the air for 12 seconds. This was long enough to prove that a heavy machine could fly—with people in it.)

Do You Have a Creative Attitude?

When you consider famous and not-so-famous creative thinkers (like the wild and crazy person who sits next to you in study hall), you probably recognize some traits they have in common. One of the most obvious is a *creative attitude*.

Whether people "look" creative on the outside isn't important. Some creative thinkers are creative dressers; others could care less what they wear, as long as they don't get arrested. It's what goes on *inside* their heads that counts.

How many of these characteristics do you share?

▶ **Creative thinkers dare to be different.** They're true risk-takers who not only *accept* uncertainty, but actually *thrive* on it. They prefer working on the edge to working at the center.

▶ **Creative thinkers are self-motivated and have a positive self-image.** They meet challenges optimistically and feel good about themselves and their accomplishments. They ignore people who tell them, "It'll never work!"" Peer pressure and group pressure don't faze them in the least.

▶ **Creative thinkers enjoy working on problems—the harder, the better.** They're happiest when facing complex problems and searching for many alternate solutions. They consider many possibilities and outcomes. They may become totally absorbed in their task—ignoring the time, skipping meals, and forgetting to sleep while they're working.

Picture the creative thinkers you know. How are they different from most other people?

*"A thought that sometimes makes me hazy:
Am I or are the others crazy?"*

Albert Einstein

Invisible Fences

Not everyone finds it easy to open up and think creatively. Sometimes "invisible fences"—mental blocks—get in the way.

Some of the most common invisible fences include:

- being afraid to make a mistake
- being afraid of criticism
- being afraid of being laughed at
- being afraid of losing friends.

Notice that they all involve *fear* of some kind. These fears are natural and may never disappear completely.

But positive thinking can help you to overcome them. (To refresh your mind about positive thinking, turn back to pages 75–77.)

- ❏ Instead of thinking, "I don't want to make a mistake," think, "A mistake may teach me something."

- ❏ Instead of thinking, "I hope no one criticizes me," think, "I will try to accept criticism and learn from it."

- ❏ Instead of thinking, "I don't want people to laugh at me," think, "I'm going to have the last laugh!"

- ❏ Instead of thinking, "I hope I won't lose any friends," think, "My *real* friends will support me and encourage me, even if they don't understand what I'm doing!"

Some invisible fences are the result of pattern thinking. While pattern thinking can be beneficial, as you learned on pages 71–72, getting in a rut can slow you down. The mind tends to focus on tried-and-true patterns because they're comfortable and don't require any effort to understand. Breaking a pattern can stretch your thinking and lead to solutions that once seemed impossible.

Take a look at this dot pattern. Now, without lifting your pencil from the paper or doing any retracing, draw four straight lines that pass through all nine dots. (P.S. If this is a library book and not your own personal copy, please *copy* the dots on a piece of paper before trying to connect them!)

●   ●   ●

●   ●   ●

●   ●   ●

Most people have a tough time solving this problem. When they look at the dots, they see a square—a square that *isn't really there*. The sides of the nonexistent square pen them in like an invisible fence.

If you have trouble connecting the dots, try thinking of them in this way: They are floating in a two-dimensional space. There are no boundaries at the top, bottom, or sides. Does this make a difference? If you still can't connect the dots, turn to page 114 for the solution.

Another invisible fence that gets in the way of creative thinking is the "one-right-answer" attitude. We all learn this in school to some degree. Multiple-choice tests allow for "one right answer." Teachers ask oral questions and expect "one right answer."

Where would we be today if the great inventors of the world had all been searching for "one right answer"? In reality, there are often *many* solutions to the same problem.

A lot of schools emphasize *convergent thinking*—pulling facts together to find "one right answer." You use convergent thinking to answer questions like these:

◐ What is the capital of Illinois?

◐ Who wrote the United States national anthem?

◐ How many pints are in a gallon?

◐ Who invented the cotton gin?

The opposite of convergent thinking is *divergent thinking,* which permits several possible answers. Divergent thinking is creative, imaginative thinking. There are no "wrong" answers. You use divergent thinking to solve problems like these:

??? How many uses can you think of for a wooden spoon?

??? Look at these 12 squares. What can you do with them?

Convergent thinking isn't necessarily "bad," and divergent thinking isn't necessarily "good." In fact, creative thinkers use *both* kinds to solve problems and generate new ideas. Divergent thinking lets the ideas come; convergent thinking verifies them.

Enhancing Your Creativity

Some people seem to think creatively with almost no effort. In fact, creative thinking takes hard work and commitment. But, as any creative thinker will tell you, it can also be a lot of fun!

Studies seem to indicate that people can become more creative if they put their minds to it. One of the first people to suggest that creativity is part of the intellect was J.P. Guilford. He was interested in learning how creativity develops, so he studied the divergent thinking process. What he found was a way to describe creative thinking in terms of four creative "products": *fluency, flexibility, originality,* and *elaboration.*

1. Fluency leads to the generation of a large number of ideas. Brainstorming—and making lists of brainstormed ideas—is one way to become more fluent. *Example:* List as many uses as you can for a soda straw.

2. Flexibility requires a variety of thought categories and the ability to shift from one category to another to generate more ideas. *Example:* Use the word "light"—and its different meanings—to come up with as many sentences as you can.

3. Originality leads to clever and unique ideas. It's difficult to define, because everyone has his or her own opinion of what it means. It's not very common, and often it seems like the result of pure chance or luck. *Example:* Think of how the world would be different if people had two heads, or if grass was pink instead of green.

4. Elaboration is the process of building on ideas or solutions by expanding them, adding details, and refining them. *Example:* How could you combine a can opener and a calculator to produce a new invention? What would your creation do?

Chances are, you've already done exercises like these in school. That's terrific! Keep practicing creative thinking, and you're bound to become more fluent, flexible, original, and elaborate.

Twenty Ways to Become More Creative than You Already Are

1. Spend time with creative people.

2. Write down your ideas so you can't lose them.

3. Laugh! Enhance your sense of humor, too. Read cartoon books. Watch comedy programs. Tell jokes with your friends. Ask somebody to tickle you.

4. Assume that anything is possible. Fantasize.

5. List everything positive about yourself that you can think of. Example: "I get along well with other people."

6. Ask "What If" questions—the crazier, the better. (What if the sky was red? What if people had only one eye, like the Cyclops? What if ants were larger than humans? What if lakes were made of chocolate?)

7. Make up similes and metaphors. Use these as jumping-off places. (A brain is like a bank—you can only take out as much as you put in. Riding a bike is like....Taking a test is like....)

8. Design new inventions to solve messy problems. (For tips, see the next section.)

9. Play "Just Suppose." (Just suppose I decided to run for class president....Just suppose I came up with a new way to clean the bird cage....Just suppose....)

10. Pay attention to so-called "small" ideas. That's where many big ideas get their start.

11. Look for different ways to express your creativity. Try painting, cooking, photography, writing, playing tennis, inventing, graffiti, etc.

12. Daydream. Let your mind wander.

13. If you're right-handed, try using your left hand to do things. If you're left-handed, switch to your right hand for a while.

14. Play strategy games like chess, backgammon, Othello, or bridge.

15. Stand on your head to get the blood really flowing to your brain.

16. Estimate and guess at measurements rather than using a yardstick, a tape measure, or a measuring cup.

17. Do your math homework *without* a calculator.

18. Read the first half of a story, then stop. Write an exciting ending of your own.

19. Make lists. Then make more lists. (List as many words as you can think of that end in "ment." List all the dogs you know by name.)

20. Imagine that your brain is like a locked door, and only *you* hold the key. Now put the key in the lock, turn it, and....

Inventing

With all that creativity stuffed inside your brain, how can you put it to use? Luckily, there are lots of ways. For example, have you ever tried inventing something to make your life or someone else's life easier? Maybe you made mental connections and linked ideas together to come up with your invention. Maybe you worked hard to make it work.

That's just how real inventors do it. They use their intuition, experience, and thinking skills to come up with ideas. They take risks and chances. They aren't afraid to be different. Does this sound familiar to you?

Anytime you decide to do something new, like create an original invention, you've actually begun to expand the networks in your brain—and increase your brain power.

Inventors usually develop their own unique styles, but the great inventors seem to have certain characteristics in common. They tend to be hard-working, curious, and driven by a desire to make improvements in the world. Plus they usually keep detailed records and visualize and/or sketch what they see in their minds. Their knowledge comes from their ability to draw conclusions from what they *can* see as well as what they *can't* see.

Most important, inventors are able to endure many failures along the way. Did you know that Thomas Edison experimented with 1,500 different filaments for the light bulb before finding the right one? When an assistant asked him how he felt about so many "failures," Edison answered, "They weren't failures. We now know 1,500 light bulb filaments that don't work."

Some famous discoveries and inventions happened by accident, like the potato chip and rubber tires. Some inventive people linked ideas that didn't seem to go together at all.

★ In 1948, George de Mestral, a Swiss engineer, was climbing in the Alps when he noticed that burrs were sticking to his clothing. As he pulled them off, he saw how the tiny hooks on each burr clung to the thread loops on the fabric. He decided to invent a fastener that would stick like a burr. It took him eight years, but he finally did it. Today his invention, called Velcro, is used in jackets, tennis shoes, spacesuits, and artificial hearts.

★ Noah Bucher of St. Paul, Minnesota, was only nine years old when he invented a new kind of underwear. While folding the laundry, he noticed a hole in a pair of his long johns. Instead of mending the hole, he tore it some more. Then he pulled the ripped long johns over his head upside-down, stuck his arms through the legs, and went to show his mom. His colorful "Topp Drawers" were sold in stores across the nation.

If you're interested in "trying on the shoes" of a real inventor, start with these playful and challenging exercises:

★ **Brainstorm!** Think about new uses for common objects like a pop can, coat hanger, or tennis ball. The possibilities are endless.

★ **Combine unrelated ideas to come up with new and useful ideas.** Burrs and fabric don't seem to have anything in common, but George de Mestral put them together and saw Velcro.

★ **Create some analogies.** How is a _____ like a _____?

Once you've tried these warm-ups, you're ready to begin.

Seven Steps to Your Own Invention

1. Think of a need or a problem you would like to solve.

2. Brainstorm as many solutions as you can.

3. Using a set of criteria (What would cost the least? Be most practical? Be easiest to produce? etc.), select a solution. This will become your invention.

4. Draw and describe your invention.

5. Construct a working model of your invention.

6. Test your invention.

7. Evaluate your invention, based on your test results. Make improvements and adjustments.

Have you ever taken an invention class? Then you know how much fun it is. If you haven't taken a class, you may want to start an Invention Club at your school. Talk to a teacher who might be interested in sponsoring your club and helping you to organize it. A local Invention Fair could turn into an annual event. Or research one of the popular national contests that are held annually for student inventors. For more information, write to: INVENT AMERICA! P.O. Box 26065, Alexandria, Virginia 22313.

SCAMPER: A Creative Thinking Checklist

Another way to enhance your creativity is by using a checklist called SCAMPER. SCAMPER is an acronym for a series of thinking processes. It was developed by Bob Eberle, a well-known author of activity books for gifted kids. He based his idea on an earlier checklist from a book by Alex Osborn called *Applied Imagination: Principles and Procedures of Creative Problem Solving.* (See how one idea can lead to another?)

When you use the SCAMPER checklist, you start with a particular object or idea in mind, then think about ways to change it. Here's what the acronym stands for:

S   **Substitute:** What could be used instead?

C   **Combine:** What could be added?

A   **Adapt:** How can it be adjusted to suit a condition or purpose?

M   **Modify:** How can the color, shape, or form be changed?
    Magnify: How can it be made larger, stronger, or thicker?
    Minify: How can it be made smaller, lighter, or shorter?

P   **Put to other uses:** What else can it be used for?

E   **Eliminate:** What can be removed or taken away from it?

R   **Reverse:** How can it be turned around or placed opposite its original position?
    Rearrange: How can the pattern, sequence, or layout be changed?

SCAMPER in Action

Imagine that you're thinking of an umbrella. Here are some ways to SCAMPER it.

Substitute: Use a wire coat hanger and plastic wrap or a plastic bag.

Combine: Add a digital clock and radio inside the umbrella handle.

Adapt: Make a version for joggers who run in the rain. It should be lightweight, glow in the dark, and easy to attach around the whole body.

Modify: Make it out of a material that dries instantly.

Magnify: Make it wide enough to keep two adults dry, or deep enough to cover one person to the knees.

Minify: Make it lighter (use a styrofoam handle?). Or make it small enough to fold up and fit inside a purse.

Put to other uses: Dig holes with it.

Eliminate: Take away the handle and attach the umbrella to a headband. Or prop it on a chair and use it as a sunshade.

Reverse: Turn it upside down, hang it on a tree, and fill it with birdseed.

Rearrange: Put the handle on the side.

"The human mind, once stretched to a new idea, never goes back to its original dimensions."

Oliver Wendell Holmes, physician, educator, author, and poet

1. Solutions to the problem on page 100, "What is 1/2 of 13?"
- ■ 1, 2, 3, 6.5, 8, and 11.
- ■ Half of 13 is 6.5 (this one is easy!)
- ■ 1/3 (the number 13 divided in half) gives you 1 and 3
- ■ X̶I̶I̶I̶ (13 in Roman numerals, divided in half) equals VIII, or 8
- ■ XI/II (XIII "divided" in half) gives you 11 and 2

How many more solutions can you find?

2. Solution to the Connect-the-Dots problem on page 104:

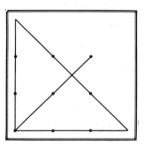

TLC FOR YOUR BRAIN

Think of the many things you take care of: your pet, bike, clothes, books, souvenirs, stuffed animals, baseball cards, collections, photographs, teeth, bedroom stereo or CD player, Rollerblades, Walkman, tapes....We take care of things so they'll stay in good shape and last longer.

Because your brain is something you can't see or touch, it's easy to forget that it needs the same TLC (Tender Loving Care) that you give to your other valuable possessions. (Also, you've had it forever, so you probably take it for granted.)

In fact, your brain needs *extra special attention* from you, because once it's damaged, it can't be fixed. It's not like a flat tire or a chipped tooth. The number of brain cells you have now is the same number you were born with, and you can't grow any more. So the trick is to keep the ones you have in tip-top condition.

How? By giving your brain regular workouts. You've heard the old saying "use it or lose it." The more you use your brain, the less brain power you'll lose as you get older. Actually, your intelligence can keep on growing far into your old age. Remember that learning creates new links between the neurons in you brain. If you never stop learning, your brain will continue forming those important new connections.

The acronym RED can help you remember to take care of your brain. It stands for **R**est, **E**xercise, and **D**iet.

Rest: Give Your Brain a Break

Rest is essential to your body *and* your brain. Your body runs on a daily "action or rest" cycle. It uses the time when you're asleep to replace old cells with new ones. Disrupting this cycle can interfere with the growth process. It can also affect your brain's rhythms.

Like your body, your brain uses your "down time" to replenish itself. While you dream, your brain generates chemicals and proteins to replace those you used up while you were awake.

You should also take study breaks and rest during the day. Your brain is under a lot of stress! Kids today are exposed to louder noises and more stimuli than ever before. Rock music, traffic, airplanes, telephones ringing, televisions blaring—they all add up. (Did you know that the average child watches 25,000 TV commercials per year?) Processing these stimuli takes a massive mental effort. That's why it's important to spend some time each day doing nothing. Kick back, close your eyes, and shut out the world. Give your overworked brain the chance to slow down.

One good way to do this is by meditating. Some people choose to learn this skill by studying Transcendental Meditation (TM) or taking classes in other forms of meditation. But you can also teach yourself the basics.

I. Find a comfortable, quiet place to sit down— an over-stuffed chair, or your bed (with pillows at your back).

2. Close your eyes and take several slow, deep breaths. Establish this as your "breathing pattern" during your meditation session.

3. Focus on relaxing every part of your body, starting with your feet and working up. (You may even want to say to yourself, "Feet, relax...Ankles, relax...Calves, relax...Knees, relax...Thighs, relax..." and so on.) By the time you get to "Head, relax," you should feel a release of tension.

4. If you like, make up your own "mantra." A mantra is a word or phrase you repeat over and over in your mind. It can be anything—nonsense syllables, your own name, a word like "umbrella." In do-it-yourself meditation, the point of a mantra is to block out any outside noises and your "inner voice."

5. Keep breathing deeply and saying your mantra (if you're using one) for a period of time that feels right to you—10 minutes, 15 minutes, half an hour, or whatever. (You may get so laid-back that you fall asleep!)

Most people who meditate claim that it not only relaxes them but also fills them with energy. Calming your mind can increase your memory capacity, improve your problem-solving abilities, and enhance your creativity, so it's certainly worth a try. You may want to schedule a regular time each day for your meditation. Or take a "meditation break" whenever you're feeling extra stressed—like during exam time.

Exercise: Get Moving!

It's no secret that the fitness craze is helping many people lead healthier, happier lives. In fact, regular physical exercise can boost your brain power. One study of schoolchildren in Canada showed that kids who exercised daily got higher grades.

Exercise can also increase your imagination and make you feel better about yourself. If you don't believe this, ask a jogger! People who jog or swim regularly talk about the good feelings they get from vigorous exercise. That's because their busy bodies are producing chemicals called *endorphins*. These natural "mind drugs" may be responsible for the "runner's high" some people experience. Highly trained athletes can feel their endorphins "kick in" while they are in motion.

If you have ever watched the Olympics or other world-class athletic competitions, you may have noticed that the athletes have a lot of energy. This is no accident. Many of them use the "taper technique." They train hard for a meet or competition, then gradually "taper off" their workouts. When their big day arrives, they have plenty of energy stored up and can perform at their peak level. You might try the taper technique to prepare for a final exam or some other mental contest, like writing a long paper. If it works for successful athletes, it may do the trick for you.

I. A month or so before your mental contest, start exercising on a regular basis. Vigorous exercise like jogging, swimming, or biking works best—*not* golf or bowling. It's important to work up a sweat!

2. About two weeks before your mental contest, give it all you've got. Exercise hard for a few days.

3. Start tapering off a little each day. Your goal is to *not* be physically active for a day or two before your mental contest.

Getting hooked on regular exercise can make a big difference for your mind. The key word here is *regular*. Occasional outbursts of activity won't be very valuable in the long run.

Exercise not only burns fat and gets your body into shape, it also helps your heart and lungs to function better and last longer.

- **Aerobic exercise** is essential to your cardiorespiratory system (your heart and lungs). Examples: jogging, walking (at a clip, *not* a stroll), swimming, bicycling, the aerobics class at your local Y.

- **Stretching and repetition exercises** ("reps") are important to your flexibility and muscle tone. Examples: yoga, pushups and situps, Nautilus exercise, lifting weights.

What's the best way to form the exercise habit? By starting *today*, not tomorrow. Make a regular exercise plan for the week and follow it faithfully. In almost no time, you'll feel more alert and energetic.

Diet: Food for Thought

What enters your body through your mouth can directly affect your thinking. Unfortunately, eating a balanced diet isn't easy for kids on the go. Sometimes it's quickest to skip a meal or grab a candy bar for a quick dose of energy. But this won't do much for your mind or your body.

Today, scientists are learning more and more about the relationship between different foods and the brain. They have discovered ways to "feed" your mind that lead to better mental performance. Let's look first at what *not* to do and why.

You come home from school hungry. Rather than reaching for good-for-you food, you munch your favorite candy bar. The sugar enters your bloodstream quickly and stimulates your brain to produce a chemical called *serotonin*. The serotonin relaxes you as it quiets the electrical signals between your brain cells. In fact, your mental performance may actually slow down—which isn't what you want to happen just before you start your homework.

Don't worry: Not all sugar is bad for you. Your brain works better if it gets a gradual flow of energy. But don't always turn to candy, sugary drinks, or other sweets. Fruit is a natural source of sugar. Let an apple energize you.

What did you eat for breakfast this morning? Did you even have time for breakfast? Maybe you were busy looking for your other Nike or your math assignment. That's no excuse for skipping breakfast! Going to school on an empty stomach is like driving a car with an almost empty gas tank. Your brain needs fuel to run on. You can't expect peak performance without it.

One study at the University of Texas showed how important breakfast is. Researchers gave a test to students at 8:00 a.m. and discovered that those who had eaten a good breakfast got much higher scores than those who had not.

What exactly is a "good breakfast"? Obviously, donuts or toaster pastries won't do as much for your brain as higher-protein foods like cheese, eggs, meat, or pizza. (Yes, pizza. Even cold, it can taste great.) Studies reveal that protein foods are an essential part of any meal. And this means more than just meat-and-potatoes. Your mind and body need lots of different foods to get the 44 nutrients known to be necessary for your health.

No matter what fast-food chains may claim, the best place to find these nutrients isn't in their burgers and fries. Most fast foods are heavy meals that contain a lot of fat. Fat is hard to digest. It keeps blood in the stomach area and away from the brain, making it that much harder to concentrate.

How can you feed your brain the best possible foods? Follow these general guidelines:

- Stick to fresh, natural foods: fruits, vegetables, grains, beans, leafy greens. They contain vitamins which help you to breathe better and increase your alertness.

- Avoid foods that have been "tampered with"—those that contain added sugars, starches, artificial flavors and preservatives.

- Avoid alcohol and other drugs, including caffeine (found in many carbonated drinks—read the labels). These may make you feel more "awake" for a while, but it's just an illusion. Too much can lead to mental dullness (or worse).

- Eat regular, healthful meals and include a variety of foods in your daily diet.

Anything you eat will eventually "go to your head." To improve your thinking, think before you eat!

If you want to find out more about food and the brain, read:

** *Care and Feeding of the Brain* by Jack Maguire (New York: Doubleday, 1990).

BIOFEEDBACK AND HYPNOSIS

⚡ A famous Tibetan yogi could sit in the snow and generate enough body heat to melt a circle around himself.

⚡ A person in an experiment raised the temperature in his right hand by visualizing himself touching a hot stove. At the same time, he lowered the temperature in his left hand by visualizing himself squeezing an ice cube.

What did these people have that you don't?

a) Special abilities

b) Supernatural powers

c) Bionic implants

d) None of the above

The answer is "none of the above." All these two men had was *knowledge* of how their bodies work. Almost anyone with that knowledge can learn to control certain bodily functions. If you wanted to, you could probably learn how to lower your blood pressure, change your body temperature, reduce your heart rate, or alter your brain waves.

Brains, Trains, and Biofeedback

Biofeedback is one way to learn about what's happening inside your body. "Feedback" means "information returned to itself." Biofeedback involves hooking yourself up to a biofeedback machine—a type of electronic equipment—that translates your bodily functions into sounds or signals. For example, a certain sound from the machine might indicate that your heart is beating too fast. A light might show what kinds of brain waves you're producing.

Dr. Barbara Brown, a brain researcher, designed a unique and exciting experiment involving biofeedback. The test subjects—children—wore electrodes on their heads that led to a brain wave monitor. The monitor in turn was connected to an electric train set. Whenever the children's brains produced alpha waves, the train moved! Experiments like these demonstrate the partnership between mind and body.

Biofeedback is sometimes used in treating illnesses. It's been estimated that 75 percent of all illnesses are related to stress. Ulcers, headaches, sore throats, and even heart attacks have been traced back to stress. Using biofeedback, people can learn to quiet their minds and relieve their stress-related aches and pains.

Although biofeedback offers new possibilities for self-improvement and body control, it hasn't yet established itself as a science. Some experts have written it off as a fad; others believe that its benefits have been exaggerated. Still others point out that inadequate equipment and stray signals can affect the biofeedback process and lead to wrong conclusions. Even so, many hospitals and universities use biofeedback in treating patients and doing research.

The jury is still out on whether biofeedback is a valid tool, but it does seem to have many potential uses. For now, we know that it can measure what's happening inside us, and that takes us one step closer to understanding ourselves.

"You Are Getting Very Sleepy...."

Can a stranger approach you on the street, quickly hypnotize you, and force you to rob a bank? Of course not! Even so, hypnosis has gotten a bad name in some circles, mostly because people don't understand it.

Used correctly, hypnosis can help people overcome problems ranging from phobias to bad habits like nail-biting and smoking. It has been effectively used in medicine in a number of ways. Hypnotized women have delivered babies by caesarean section (surgery) without an anesthetic. Hypnotized people have gone through dental surgery without drugs.

When you're hypnotized, you enter an altered state of consciousness. You may seem to be asleep, or you may seem to be wide awake and alert. There are many different levels of hypnotic "sleep."

Most people can be hypnotized; in fact, about 90 percent of young people can be put into a very deep trance. But they can't be hypnotized without their consent. In fact, hypnosis won't "take" if you don't trust the hypnotist and aren't willing to cooperate.

Trained hypnotists use several methods to put people in trances. They may persuade their subjects to relax and block out distracting thoughts. They may ask them to feel their arms, legs, and eyelids getting heavy ("you are getting very sleepy..."). They may use something called "sensory monotony"—having people stare at an object for a period of time. They may use visualization or imagery.

Hypnotized people have performed amazing feats, from lifting large, heavy objects to painting beautiful pictures. It's likely that the physical and mental capabilities needed to perform those feats were already there, and that hypnotism merely released them.

One characteristic common to all forms of hypnosis is a "directed link" between one level of consciousness and another. Hypnosis moves you out of the level you're at to another level you may not be able to get to on your own. Psychologists believe that there may be as many as 20 different states of consciousness.

Hypnosis can have positive results, but there are still unanswered questions—and genuine concerns—about its use. Nobody quite understands what happens when a person is hypnotized. Maybe someday someone will invent a way to measure brain waves, pulse rates, skin responses, and eye movements of people in a trance. Until then, hypnosis will probably remain a mystery.

Hypnosis isn't for amateurs, and it doesn't work for everyone. Inducing a trance may seem simple, but getting someone out of a trance can be difficult. Some people have stayed in a trance long after being hypnotized. Others have suffered emotional aftereffects. That's why *only qualified and trained professionals should perform hypnosis.* It's not a party game!

Serious hypnosis isn't something you should play with. But you can practice a mild form of *self-hypnosis* to help you relax and get in touch with your inner feelings. Self-hypnosis is a safe, effective means of finding out more about yourself. If there's a particular goal you want to achieve, or if you want to improve yourself in some other way, it's worth a try.

Hypnosis consultant Frank Shams recommends this two-step technique for beginning your self-hypnosis routine:

1. Find a quiet room and a comfortable place to sit.

2. Close your eyes and mentally count backwards *slowly* from 50 to 0.

When you reach 0, you'll probably be in a light hypnotic state. (Even if you're not, you'll be more relaxed than you were when you started. This exercise is also a great tension reliever.)

What can you do with your newfound ability? You may want to use it to solve a problem you've been having. For example, let's say you bite your nails. You've made several attempts to quit, but you haven't had any success. So you decide to try self-hypnosis. Here's what you might do:

1. On a 3" x 5" card, write, "I want to stop biting my nails."

2. Read the card silently three times.

3. Now go into your light hypnotic state.

4. Once you're there, visualize yourself as a person who isn't a nail-biter. Talk to yourself softly but firmly.

5. When you feel that this message has gotten through to your subconscious, stop.

6. Gradually come out of your hypnotic state. You may want to take some deep breaths and do a few stretches.

Whenever you're able to visualize a goal and mentally act it out, you increase your chances of success. Naturally, it's important to choose a *realistic* goal. No matter how many times you repeat to yourself, "I want to sprout wings and fly," it's not going to happen!

SLEEP AND DREAMS

In 1968, Bertha van der Merwe of Capetown, South Africa, went without sleep for 11 days, 18 hours, and 55 minutes. She set the world's record.

In 1959, a New York disk jockey named Peter Tripp stayed awake for 200 hours (that's more than 8 days) as a publicity stunt to raise money for charity.

For most people, these kinds of sleepless marathons are nearly impossible. Forty-eight hours are usually enough to make us feel weird and act strange. (Tripp had wild hallucinations. He thought he saw a friend's face on a clock dial, a fire in his dresser drawer, and a suit growing fuzzy worms!)

People who are deprived of sleep become grouchy, confused, and accident-prone. They have a tough time doing their jobs or schoolwork. The fact is, we *need* sleep. One reason is because the human body operates on a 24-hour cycle. Our "body clock" functions according to Circadian (24-hour) rhythms that correspond to certain hours of the day.

Every person's body clock is unique. Most people need about 8 hours of sleep per day and spend the other

16 on waking activities. Others seem to require less sleep (as little as 4-5 hours) or more (as much as 10 hours).

Another reason people need sleep is because the body uses those hours to make internal repairs. Still another reason may be due to "genetic programming." Our long-ago ancestors slept at night because it was too dangerous to hunt in the dark. Maybe our DNA remembers.

Scientists don't know precisely why we need sleep, but they have a pretty good idea of what happens when we do drop off.

The Four Stages of Sleep

People used to believe that not much went on in the brain during sleep. Wrong! While you're out cold, parts of your brain are wide awake.

Researchers in sleep labs study sleeping people to learn what happens in both the mind and the body. They use several special instruments, the most common being the electroencephalograph, or EEG. Being hooked up to an EEG is a painless procedure. Electrodes are simply taped to parts of the body. Wires run from the electrodes into the EEG and carry messages to it. The EEG records these messages as lines on a long roll of paper. A readout from a single night might be 1,500 feet long!

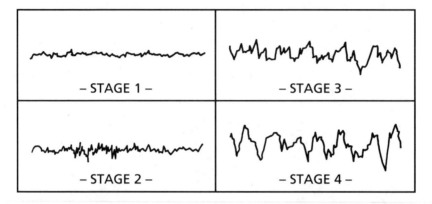

– STAGE 1 –	– STAGE 3 –
– STAGE 2 –	– STAGE 4 –

The EEG tells the researchers about the different stages of sleep. Your brain travels back and forth between these stages all night long.

Stage 1: Drifting off to sleep. Your muscles relax. Your body temperature drops. You heart slows down. You may squirm around and change positions. (In a single night, you may change positions as often as 30 times.)

Stage 2: Light sleep. You may keep squirming around. Since you're not yet "sound asleep," you may be easily awakened.

Stage 3: Deep sleep. Your blood pressure drops. You're not as easy to wake up.

Stage 4: Deepest sleep. You may talk in your sleep or even walk in your sleep. It's very difficult to wake you up.

Typically, you stay in stage 4 for a few minutes, then move back through stages 3 and 2 and finally to stage 1. At this point, you may start to dream, and keep dreaming for about 20 minutes. Then you go back down through stages 2, 3, and 4. This up-down, yo-yo pattern continues throughout the night. As morning approaches, your dreams last longer and your deep-sleep stages are shorter.

Dreams and Nightmares

Dreaming sleep is much more interesting than regular sleep. Scientists who study sleep have learned that dreamers' eyes move back and forth as if they're watching an exciting movie. This phenomenon is called REM, for **R**apid **E**ye **M**ovement.

When you're in REM sleep, your heart beats faster and your breathing is heavier than usual. If you're suddenly awakened, you'll almost certainly be able to remember what you were dreaming about.

■ ■ ■ ■ ■ ■ ■ ■ ■ ■ ■ ■ ■ ■ ■ ■ ■

DREAM FACTS

◆ About one-third of dreams take place in houses; one-fourth are set in buses, cars, boats, trains, and other moving vehicles.

◆ People dream in color but usually remember their dreams in black-and-white.

◆ 40 percent of dreams are about strangers—people unknown to the dreamers.

■ ■ ■ ■ ■ ■ ■ ■ ■ ■ ■ ■ ■ ■ ■ ■ ■

Most dreams occur in familiar settings and involve events that happened during the daylight (or waking) hours. We dream about food, friends, and family members, teachers, romance, problems, sporting events, tests, conversations, abstract ideas—anything and everything. Usually we don't have any control over what goes on in our dreams (but some people claim that they do).

Maybe you never remember your dreams. This doesn't mean that you don't dream. In fact, *everybody* dreams. So do dogs, cats, and other mammals. (You've probably seen your dog "chasing cats" in its sleep. Its paws may twitch, and it may even growl or bark.)

REM sleep occurs approximately every 90 minutes. You spend a total of about two hours every night in this dreaming, "active" sleep state. If you miss out on it one night, your brain will "catch up" on the next. Over your lifetime, you'll spend from four to six years just dreaming.

Modern dream experts say that our dreams speak to us in symbols, paradoxes, and riddles. Psychiatrists and psychologists sometimes try to help people interpret their dreams and uncover their meanings.

Dreams may be a way of reviewing what happens in our lives and sorting out the things we don't understand. They do seem to mirror our emotions; if we're upset, angry, frustrated, happy, or scared during the day, the same feelings might surface in the dreams we have at night.

Dreams are usually enjoyable and entertaining. We may fly, or save the world, or ace a math test, or win the heart of someone we have a crush on. But what about the times when our dreams *aren't* so pleasant? When you wake up with your heart in your mouth, a sweaty body, and a racing pulse, you know you've had a nightmare! Here's the good news: Nightmares are necessary and normal. Necessary because they act as a sort of "safety valve," giving you the opportunity to get in touch with your fears without actually putting yourself in danger. Normal because everybody has them.

Some dream experts believe that people dream about ghosts, monsters, giant animals with fangs, and creepy slimy creatures when there's a disturbance in their life. Contrary to popular belief, eating certain foods before going to bed won't give you nightmares (although a spicy enchilada at midnight could keep you awake for a while). So the next time you have a nightmare, don't blame it on the pickles!

Making Your Dreams Work for You

Are dreams a waste of time? Or can you *do* something with all the action that goes on in your head while you sleep?

z-z-z Some mathematicians claim that they have written complex equations in their sleep.

z-z-z Jack Nicklaus, a famous professional golfer, improved his golf score by practicing the way he dreamed he held his club.

z-z-z Robert Louis Stevenson based *The Strange Case of Dr. Jekyll and Mr. Hyde* on his nightmares.

z-z-z Freidrich August Kekule von Stradonitz, a German chemist, was trying to understand how carbon atoms are arranged in a molecule of a chemical called *benzene*. One day he took a nap and dreamed about six snakes biting each other's tails and whirling in circles. When he woke up, he understood the structure of the benzene ring.

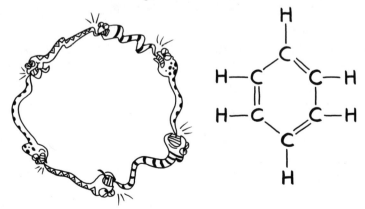

In order to use your dreams, you have to be able to remember them. This isn't always easy. People who insist that they "never dream" only think that because they never remember their dreams. Maybe you recall some of your dreams and not others. If you'd like to hold on to more, try this approach:

I. Put a notebook, pen and paper, or tape recorder next to your bed. This will be your Dream Journal.

2. Just before you drop off to sleep, "remind" yourself to dream. One way to do this is by visualizing something you want to dream about.

3. When you wake up, don't jump out of bed right away. Instead, lie still for a few moments. The details of your dream may come back to you.

4. In your Dream Journal, record as much of your dream as you can recall. Do it immediately. A dream that isn't captured quickly tends to fade away and vanish.

Some people who *really* want to remember their dreams set their alarm clocks to go off in the middle of the night. Being awakened suddenly, and at a time when you're not usually awakened, can take a dream by surprise.

You may want to keep your Dream Journal with you during the day. A word, a gesture, or a situation may bring a dream rushing back into your consciousness. Be sure to date the entries in your Dream Journal. Later, you can look back to see how your dreams have related to the events in your life. Maybe you'll find patterns, or dream series, or recurrent dreams—dreams that happen over and over again. Their meanings may not seem clear at first, but sooner or later you'll probably make discoveries about yourself.

**"All that we see or seem
is but a dream within a dream."**

Edgar Allan Poe, American poet and story writer,
whose stories are among the scariest ever written

Mind Cycles

Would you rather take an important test at 8:00 a.m., 11:00 a.m., or 3:00 p.m.? Maybe you're a night owl who performs best at midnight. Each of us has a favorite time of day when we prefer to do our heaviest mental work. That time is determined by our body clock, which is affected by the cycles of the Earth itself.

One of our most basic cycles is waking and sleeping. But many other cycles occur within the body each day. Our body temperature, heart rate, blood pressure, perspiration rate, and hormone levels are constantly adjusting themselves. (Your body clock is regulated by your hypothalamus, which you read about on page 11.)

Most humans are at their best during the day. But a few nocturnal types are more efficient while the rest of us are sound asleep in our beds. To get the most mileage out of your brain, it helps to know your peak times and slump times. One way to find out is by taking your temperature. Body heat corresponds to mental alertness. So the warmer you are, the sharper your mind is.

Our bodies try to maintain a pattern of waking and sleeping. That's why you probably feel tired and lazy after a slumber party or other late-night activity. When you lose sleep, your body is forced to shift into a new mini-cycle. It may seem as if you have jet lag—that strange sensation of not really knowing what time it is.

How do you feel when you return to class after lunch? Do you ever wish you could take a nap? You're not alone. Researchers have discovered that a midday drop in alertness is a biological response to our human need to relax after lunch. In many countries, businesses literally "close up shop" for several hours during the afternoon. People enjoy long rests or leisurely lunches. Maybe you should try taking a *siesta* sometime. See how it affects your alertness for the rest of the day.

You may have heard that you perform better in the morning, when your mind is "fresh." This isn't necessarily true. One researcher found that the likelihood of making errors is *greater* in the morning than in the afternoon. On the other hand, we tend to be speedier in the morning. So it seems that we have a choice: to be quicker and less accurate in the morning, or slower and more accurate in the mid-afternoon.

What can we do with what we know about body rhythms? You may want to try to discover your personal peak time of day. When are you at your best? From there, you can figure out ways to take advantage of this important time.

If you want to know more about dreams and dreaming, read:

* *Dreams Can Help: A Journal Guide to Understanding Your Dreams and Making Them Work for You* by Jonni Kincher (Minneapolis: Free Spirit Publishing Inc., 1988).

** *Dream Work* by Jeremy Taylor (New York: Paulist Press, 1983).

MYSTERIES OF THE MIND

Did you ever dream about something that later came true? Did you ever hear the telephone ring and *know* who was calling, even before you picked up the receiver? Did you ever have the eerie feeling that you had already met someone you were meeting for the first time? Did you ever feel sure that you were "reading" another person's mind?

We all experience odd coincidences in our lives. But are they purely accidental? Or is it possible that something really big is going on?

Carl Jung coined the term *synchronicity* to describe coincidences that seem meaningful but have no apparent cause. He believed that these "meaningful coincidences" had their basis in the "collective unconscious"— humankind's shared experiences. Maybe, he suggested, people's unconscious minds were somehow linked with one another.

So far, this is pure speculation. But there does appear to be evidence that the mind perceives the world in ways that the senses do not.

What are the boundaries of the mind? Can these boundaries be transcended? Can the mind go beyond the senses—and beyond time and space? Does the brain give off some kind of physical "energy" that can be detected and decoded? These are fascinating questions that don't yet have answers. We still don't know enough about the brain and how it works. But it can be fun—and challenging—to speculate on the mysteries of the mind.

If you're interested in finding out more about unexplained phenomena of the mind, try researching the topic of *parapsychology*. Read what people have to say about ESP, telepathy, and other interesting subjects. Just be aware that they can arouse people's emotions and prejudices. Although parapsychology has intrigued human beings for centuries, there are some who get upset about anything having to do with these "mysteries of the mind."

Most of the research going on today doesn't try to prove the existence of these phenomena one way or the other. Instead, it explores the possibility that we can learn to develop and use our "mental powers" in our everyday lives. Remember: The more we know about the mind and the brain, the more we know about ourselves.

THE MYSTERIOUS BRAIN

WHAT'S NEXT?

As you read through this book, what were your thoughts? Did you think about ways to use this information to make the most of the brain you were born with? What else would you like to know about the brain? How will you go about seeking answers to your questions?

Remember that there's still a lot we *don't* know about the brain. Each day, researchers continue to piece together this complicated puzzle. It's not an easy task. But with hard work and advanced technology, we humans can keep exploring the last and greatest biological frontier: *the brain.*

"It may well be there is something else going on in the brain that we don't have an inkling of at the moment."

Roger Penrose, English physicist and author of
The Emperor's New Mind

BIBLIOGRAPHY

Albrecht, Karl. *Learn to Improve Your Thinking Skills.* Englewood Cliffs, NJ: Prentice-Hall, Inc., 1980.

Begley, Sharon, John Carey, and Ray Sawhill. "How the Brain Works," in *Newsweek* (February 7, 1983).

Begley, Sharon, Lynda Wright, Chuck Vernon, and Mary Hager. "Mapping the Brain," in *Newsweek* (April 20, 1992).

Bloom, Floyd E., Arlyne Lazerson, and Laura Hofstadter. *Brain, Mind and Behavior,* 2nd edition. New York: W.H. Freeman and Co., 1988.

Buzan, Tony. *Make the Most of Your Mind.* New York: Linden Press/Simon and Schuster, 1984.
—*Use Both Sides of Your Brain.* New York: E.P. Dutton, 1983.

Clark, Barbara. *Growing Up Gifted.* Columbus, OH: Charles E. Merrill Publishing Co., 1988.

Cohen, Daniel. *Intelligence: What Is It?* New York: M. Evans and Company, Inc., 1974.

Corrick, James A. *The Human Brain—Mind and Matter.* New York: Arco Publishing, 1983.

Eberle, Robert. *SCAMPER: Games for Imagination Development.* Buffalo, NY: D.O.K. Publishers, 1971.

Ehrenberg, Miriam, and Otto Ehrenberg, Ph.D. *Optimum Brain Power.* New York: Dodd, Mead and Co., 1985.

Ferris, Timothy. *The Mind's Sky.* New York: Bantam, 1992.

Galyean, Beverly-Colleene. "Expanding Human Intelligence," in *The Futurist* (October 1, 1983).

Gardner, Howard. *Frames of Mind: The Theory of Multiple Intelligences.* New York: Basic Books, 1983.

Hopson, Janet L. "A Magical Memory Tour," in *Psychology Today* (November, 1983).

Ornstein, Robert, and Richard F. Thompson. *The Amazing Brain.* Boston: Houghton-Mifflin Co., 1986.

Osborn, Alex. *Applied Imagination: Principles and Procedures of Creative Problem Solving.* New York: Scribners, 1963.

Restak, Richard. *The Brain.* New York: Warner Books, 1988.

Russell, Peter. *The Brain Book.* New York: E.P. Dutton, 1984.

Samuels, Michael, and Nancy Samuels. *Seeing With the Mind's Eye.* New York: Random House, 1975.

Signe, Hammer. "Stalking Intelligence: I.Q. Isn't the End of the Line—You Can Be Smarter," in *Science Digest* (June, 1985).

Silverstein, Alvin, and Virginia B. Silverstein. *The World of the Brain.* New York: Morrow Jr. Books, 1986.

Simon, Seymour. *The Optical Illusion Book.* New York: W. Morrow and Co., 1984.

Sternberg, Robert J. "Who's Intelligent?" in *Psychology Today* (April, 1982).
—"How Can We Teach Intelligence?" in *Educational Leadership* (September, 1984).

vos Savant, Marilyn. *Omni: I.Q. Quiz Contest.* New York: McGraw Hill Book Co., 1985.

Ward, Brian R. *The Brain and Nervous System.* New York: Franklin Watts, 1981.

Willing, Jules Z. *The Lively Mind.* New York: William Morrow and Co., 1982.

Yepsen, Roger. *Smarten Up!* Boston: Little, Brown and Co., 1990.

INDEX

Male brain, size of, 15, 50
vs. female brain, 50-54
and variability in intelligence,
50-51
Mantra, and meditation, 117
Mathematical thinking, left brain
control of, 45
Mathematics tests
of achievement, 32
position for taking, 79
Maturation. *See* Pituitary gland
Mead, Margaret, as genius, 55
Meditation, 116-117
Medulla oblongata, 10
Memory, 82-95
collective, 87
déjà vu, 87
eidetic, 86
and forgetting, 87-89
formation and storage, 10, 11, 13
improving, 89-93
location in brain, 83
long-term, 85
mnemonics for, 91-93
motor-skill, 86
photographic, 86
rote, 90
sensory, 85
short-term, 85
synapses and, 17
theories on, 84-85
and time of day, 91
types of, 85-87
verbal/semantic, 86
Mental age (MA), and intelligence
testing, 28, 29, 31
Mental blocks, and creativity, 103-
106
Mental strain, as memory block, 88
Messages, sent and received by
brain. *See* Electrical impulses;
Nerve impulses
Metaphorical thinking, 46
and creativity, 108
right brain control of, 46
Michelangelo, 101
Mill, John Stuart, IQ of, 30

Mind
vs. brain, 5-6
conscious vs. unconscious, 62
defined, 5
mysteries of, 138-139
Mini-brain. *See* Cerebellum
Montana, Joe, as genius, 55, 56
Mood-altering drugs, 10
Morrison, Van, 6
Mozart, Wolfgang Amadeus
as genius, 55
IQ of, 30
musical intelligence of, 42
MRI. *See* Magnetic resonance
imaging (MRI)
Multiple-choice tests, 105
Multiple intelligences. *See*
Intelligence, multiple
Muscle coordination, 12
Musical intelligence, 42
right brain control of, 46

N

Nature, vs. nurture, 37-39, 40, 53
Navratilova, Martina, and
concentration, 12
Negative thinking, 76
Neocortex, 13
Nerve impulses, 16
Neurons, 16-17, 19, 115
Neurosurgeons, and brain research,
44
New brain. *See* Cerebrum
Newton, Isaac
on gravity, 101
IQ of, 30
Nicklaus, Jack, use of dream by, 133
Nierenberg, Gerard, on using brain,
98
Nightmares. *See* Dreams
Nucleus, 17
Nurture, vs. nature, 37-39, 40, 53

O

Olympic athletes, 12, 58, 118
Optical illusions, 73-75
Originality, as product of creativity,
106-107

Sequential thinking, left brain
    control of, 45
Serotonin, 120
Shakespeare, William, on thinking
    and feeling, 79
Shams, Frank, on self-hypnosis, 127
Shereshevskii, Solomon, memory
    skill of, 82
Similes, creating, 108
Simon, Theodore, and intelligence
    testing, 28
Simultaneous processing, right
    brain control of, 46
Sixth sense. *See* Intuition
Size, of the brain, 3, 6, 7-8, 15
Sleep, 128-137
    cycles for, 136
    denying, 128
    napping, 136
    need for, 128-129
    stages of, 129-131
    See also Dreams
Smartness, vs. intelligence, 24, 33, 35
Smell, sense of, 10
Smell brain. *See* Limbic system
Sound, imagining, 64, 65
Spatial intelligence, 42
    right brain control of, 46
Speed, brain, 18
SQUID, 20, 21
Stage fright, 89
Standardized tests, 34
Stanford-Binet test, 31
Stanley, Julian, on male brain, 51
Statistics, about the brain, 6, 7
Stem, brain. *See* Brain stem
Stern, William, on mental quotient,
    28
Sternberg, Robert, on intelligence,
    24, 40-41
Stevenson, Robert Louis, use of
    dream by, 133
Stimulation, 39
*The Strange Case of Dr. Jekyll and
    Mr. Hyde* (Stevenson), 133
Strategic thinking, 78
    and creativity, 108
Stress, as memory block, 88
Stretching and repetition exercises
    (reps), 119

Success, focusing on, 75
Sugar, effect on brain, 120
Superconductivity quantum
    interference device. *See* SQUID
Symbols
    ability to understand, 13, 32
    of dreams, 132
Synapses, 17, 19

T

Tacit knowledge, 41
Talent, and creativity, 97
Talking, left brain control of, 45
Taper technique, and exercise, 118
Taste
    imagining, 65
    and smell brain, 10
Teddy bears, origin of name, 4
Terman, Lewis, and intelligence
    testing, 31
Tests
    achievement, 32
    college admissions, 34
    intelligence, 27-36
    mathematics, 32, 79
    multiple-choice, 105
    reading, 32
    standardized, 34
    Stanford-Binet, 31
Thalamus, 11
Tharp, Twyla, achievements of, 56
Thinking, 62-81
    convergent, 105-106
    divergent, 105-106
    and intelligence, 24
    kinds of, 63
    literal, 45
    logical, 66-69
    metaphorical, 46, 108
    negative, 76
    number of thoughts per day, 83
    patterns in, 46, 71-72, 83, 104
    positive, 75-77
    quick, 78
    sharpening skills, 78-79
    as skill, 63
    strategic, 78, 108
    unconscious vs. conscious, 62
Thinking cap. *See* Cerebrum

ABOUT THE AUTHOR

Susan L. Barrett received her Bachelor of Science degree in Elementary Education, and her Masters degree in Educational Psychology with emphasis on Gifted and Talented Education from the University of Wisconsin in Madison. Her interest and desire to work with gifted children began in 1981 and has continued ever since. Throughout the years, she has devoted herself to encouraging young people to recognize their unlimited potential, intelligences, and hidden talents.

Currently, Susan is the Talented and Gifted Program Coordinator for Grades K-12 in Elmhurst, Illinois. Previously, she was a resource teacher for gifted students for thirteen years in Illinois and Minnesota. Her current position allows her to remain involved in many aspects of gifted education, including staff development, differentiation of curriculum/instruction, identification, collaboration, research, and program evaluation. She has facilitated numerous workshops throughout the Midwestern states.

Susan resides in the western suburbs of Chicago with her husband, 9-year-old twin sons, and 4-year-old son. Her favorite activities include spending time with her family and "acting like a kid again." She also enjoys traveling, writing, reading, and surfing the net. In the future, Susan plans to cultivate her newfound interest in the arts and continue to share her love of learning with her children and her students.

Visit us on the Web!

www.freespirit.com

Stop by anytime to find our Parents' Choice Approved catalog with fast, easy, secure 24-hour online ordering; "Ask Our Authors," where visitors ask questions—and authors give answers—on topics important to children, teens, parents, teachers, and others who care about kids; links to other Web sites we know and recommend; fun stuff for everyone, including quick tips and strategies from our books; and much more! Plus our site is completely searchable so you can find what you need in a hurry. Stop in and let us know what you think!

Just point and click!

new! Get the first look at our books, catch the latest news from Free Spirit, and check out our site's newest features.

contact Do you have a question for us or for one of our authors? Send us an email. Whenever possible, you'll receive a response within 48 hours.

order! Order in confidence! Our secure server uses the most sophisticated online ordering technology available. And ordering online is just one of the ways to purchase our books: you can also order by phone, fax, or regular mail. No matter which method you choose, excellent service is our goal.

1.800.735.7323 • fax 612.337.5050 • help4kids@freespirit.com

Other Great Books from Free Spirit

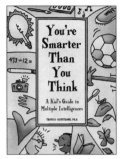

You're Smarter Than You Think
A Kid's Guide to Multiple Intelligences
by Thomas Armstrong, Ph.D.
In clear, simple language, this book introduces Howard Gardner's theory of multiple intelligences. Resources point the way to books, software, games, and organizations that can help kids develop the eight intelligences. For ages 8–12.
$15.95; 192 pp.; softcover; illus.; 7" x 9"

Psychology for Kids
40 Fun Tests That Help You Learn About Yourself
by Jonni Kincher
A creative, hands-on workbook that promotes self-discovery, self-awareness, and self-esteem and empowers young people to make good choices.
For ages 10 & up.
$16.95; 152 pp.; softcover; illus.; 8½" x 11"

Psychology for Kids II
40 Fun Experiments That Help You Learn About Others
by Jonni Kincher
Based on sound psychological concepts, these experiments make it fun and interesting for kids to learn about their families, friends, and classmates. For ages 12 & up.
$17.95; 168 pp.; softcover; illus.; 8½" x 11"

Stick Up for Yourself!
Every Kid's Guide to Personal Power
and Positive Self-Esteem
Revised and Updated Edition
by Gershen Kaufman, Ph.D., Lev Raphael, Ph.D.,
and Pamela Espeland
Simple text teaches assertiveness, responsibility, relationship skills, choice making, problem solving, and goal setting. For ages 8–12.
$11.95; 128 pp.; softcover; illus.; 6" x 9"

To place an order or to request a free catalog of
SELF-HELP FOR KIDS® *and* SELF-HELP FOR TEENS® *materials, please*
write, call, email, or visit our Web site:

Free Spirit Publishing Inc.
217 Fifth Avenue North • Suite 200 • Minneapolis, MN 55401-1299
toll-free 800.735.7323 • local 612.338.2068 • fax 612.337.5050
help4kids@freespirit.com • www.freespirit.com